SALTY
LANGUAGE

AN UNABRIDGED DICTIONARY OF MARINE CORPS SLANG, TERMS & JARGON

Compiled by MSgt A. A. Bufalo USMC (Ret)

ISBN 978-0-9745793-7-5

First Printing – June 2006
Printed in the United States of America

www.AllAmericanBooks.com

Salty Language

BOOKS BY ANDY BUFALO

SWIFT, SILENT & SURROUNDED
Sea Stories and Politically Incorrect Common Sense

THE OLDER WE GET, THE BETTER WE WERE
MORE Sea Stories and Politically Incorrect Common Sense
Book II

NOT AS LEAN, NOT AS MEAN, STILL A MARINE!
Even MORE Sea Stories and Politically Incorrect Common Sense
Book III

EVERY DAY IS A HOLIDAY...
Every Meal is a Feast!
Yet Another Book of Sea Stories and Politically Incorrect Common Sense
Book IV

THE ONLY EASY DAY WAS YESTERDAY
Marines Fighting the War on Terrorism

HARD CORPS
The Legends of the Marine Corps

AMBASSADORS IN BLUE
In Every Clime and Place
Marine Security Guards Protecting Our Embassies Around the World

HOLLYWOOD MARINES
Celebrities Who Served in the Corps

THE LORE OF THE CORPS
Quotations By, For & About Marines

PREFACE

"Salty Language" was born when a member of my Marine Corps League Detachment asked if there was a 'dictionary of Marine Corps terms' he could get for his girlfriend – since she was apparently having difficulty understanding half the things he said. I looked into it, and discovered there was nothing comprehensive (i.e. containing slang, terms, *and* jargon) and unabridged (i.e. including 'bad' words) - so I decided to put one together myself.

This book is not 'all inclusive' (that would be impossible!) but is instead designed to give the reader a fairly comprehensive grounding in Marine Corps lingo. I have also included a number of archaic terms from the 'Old Corps' for their entertainment value, as well as the names of some prominent Marines for historical purposes.

Retired Colonel James W. Hammond Jr. once wrote, "Marines are 'Soldiers of the Sea,' and it is right and proper that their conversation be sprinkled with nautical expressions... it is a matter of pride to sport a regulation haircut, spit-shined shoes, proper civilian attire and, of course, salty language. After all, it is gratifying when some stranger at a cocktail party says, 'You sound like you're a Marine.'"

So whether you are new to the Corps, a family member, or even a 'salty' Marine, there is something in this book for *you!*

Table of Contents
(Listed using the phonetic alphabet)

Salty Language

NUMERICAL TERMS

Salty Language

0 Dark 30
> See "Zero Dark Thirty."

030SHIT
> Military Occupational Specialty of a junior infantry officer (Pronounced *oh-three-oh-shit*).

0311
> Infantryman (Pronounced *oh-three-eleven*).

1631
> The "MOS" of a "Liberty Hound"; they are ready to bolt out the hatch as soon as "Liberty Call" sounds, which normally occurs at 1630 (Pronounced *sixteen-thirty-one*).

1775
> Number on the license plate of the Commandant's official vehicle; year of the Marine Corps' birth (Pronounced *seventeen-seventy-five*).

1775 Rum Punch
> Reminiscent of the "grog ration" served aboard the wooden sailing ships of the Continental Navy; traditional drink for the "Corps and Country" toast at Mess Nights; consists of four parts rum, two parts lime juice, one part maple syrup, and grenadine to taste (ice liberally).

I Corps
> One Corps; the northernmost of four corps areas in South Vietnam; was adjacent to the DMZ; I Corps was the province of the U. S. Marines, while II, III and IV Corps were U. S. Army areas (Pronounced *eye-core*).

1st CivDiv
1st Civilian Division; civilian life; life before or after service in the Marine Corps.

1-MC
Communication system aboard ship which allows orders and information to be passed immediately to all members of the crew; usually a series of speakers throughout the entire ship.

5 Paragraph Order
See "SMEAC."

8th and I
Oldest Marine Barracks; location of the Commandant's house, Marine Barracks Washington, the Marine Corps Band, the Drum and Bugle Corps and the Marine Corps Institute; it is the ceremonial home of the Corps; the only public building not set afire when the British overran Washington, D.C. during the War of 1812 - some say out of respect for the Corps' stoic defense at Bladensburg Pike; so named due to its address at the corner of 8th and I Streets SE, in Washington, D.C. (Pronounced *eighth and eye*)

12th General Order
Unofficial General Order; see "General Orders"; it reads "To walk my post from flank to flank, and take no shit from *any* rank!"

29 Palms
See "Stumps, The"

29 Stumps
See "Stumps, The"

45
.45 caliber weapon; usually the M1911A1.

72
A 72-hour liberty; granted by commanding officers; not charged as leave.

86
To throw away or get rid of something; from the number of the form originally used to remove an item from a stock record.

90-Day Wonder
Unflattering term for an OCS graduate; refers to the early practice of training commissioned officers in three months rather than the four years in the Naval Academy or the four year part-time training in ROTC; prevalent during WWII, when officers couldn't be commissioned fast enough to keep up with the demand for them in the fleet; also "90-day *blunder*."

96
A 96-hour liberty; granted by commanding officers for outstanding duty, unit successes or special holidays; not charged as leave.

782 Gear
Originally individual equipment owned by a unit and issued to a Marine while he is assigned to that unit; in boot camp that included a bucket, cleaning equipment, a poncho and a shelter half; name is

derived from the original form number used to issue equipment during WWII and Korea; present use refers to the Load Bearing Vest, cartridge belt and the equipment attached to it, as well as other field equipment; often called "deuce gear."

1000 inch Range

A rifle range of approximately 1000 inches used to "zero" weapons prior to qualification or deployment.

1369

Fictional MOS for an unlucky (13) cocksucker (69).

1900

Homosexual; from the paragraph in the Separations Manual in the 1970s and 1980s which discusses homosexuals.

2569

Fictional MOS for a two-bit (25) cocksucker (69).

Alfa

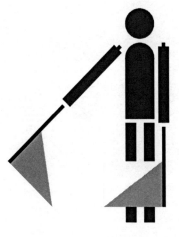

Salty Language

A-1 Sky Raider
Last propeller driven aircraft used for CAS in combat; much loved by grunts, because they could loiter over the target area and were more accurate than jets due to their relatively slow airspeed; also called "Sandy" or "Spad."

AAA
Anti-Aircraft Artillery; usually called "Triple A."

AAV
Armored Amphibious Vehicle; see "Amtrac" and "LVT."

A/O
Area of Operations.

A. J. Squared Away
A Marine with everything in place and in order; the perfect Marine; the opposite of a "Shitbird" or "Joe Shit the Rag Man."

Abaft.
Aft of any given point on a ship.

Aboard
Within the confines of a location; a Marine is not "at" or "on" a Marine Corps installation, he is a*board* it!

AC
Aircraft Commander

ACE
Air Combat Element; part of a MAGTF (pronounced *ace*).

Ace
   A combat pilot with five or more "Kills."

ACE Medical
   "Battalion Aid Station" for USMC Aviation units in the field.

Acme Beer
   World War II era beer made in San Jose, California and sent to the South Pacific specifically for Marine units; it came in both a green and a brown bottle, but only the brown colored bottles were fit to drink; the green bottles contained a liquid that smelled like a skunk.

Actual
   Radio designation for the commander of a unit; if the unit call sign is "Warlord," the unit commander would be "Warlord Actual."

AD
   Active Duty; also "Accidental Discharge"; see "Negligent Discharge."

Adjutant
   Officer who acts as military assistant to a more senior officer; staff officer in charge of and responsible for administrative functions within a unit, including correspondence and records.

Administrative Discharge
   Non-punitive discharge given prior to completion of an enlistment; a way for the Marine Corps to get rid of someone without affecting their post-service benefits.

Adrift

Floating aimlessly; without a rudder or compass; missing in action; setting one's self off from the norm.

AFRTS

Armed Forces Radio and Television System; provider of commercial-type radio and television programming to ships and overseas stations (Pronounced *a-farts*).

Aft

Behind; from the naval term for the after section of the ship.

AFU

All Fucked Up.

AH-1

See "Cobra."

Air Start

Blow job.

Air Strike

See "Close Air Support."

Air Wing

Aviation unit equivalent to an infantry division; also refers to the USMC aviation establishment as a whole.

Airdale

Anyone serving in aviation.

AK-47

Soviet-manufactured Kalashnikov semi-automatic and fully automatic combat assault rifle, 7.62-mm; the basic weapon of Communist forces, third world countries and terrorists; made famous in the movie "Heartbreak Ridge."

Albany

MCLB located in Albany GA.

ALCON

All concerned; used in radio traffic.

Ali Baba

Middle Eastern enemy combatant; a looter, or any bad guy; from "Ali Baba and the 40 Thieves"; first used during OIF.

All Hands

Everyone.

ALICE

All-purpose Lightweight Individual Carrying Equipment; a load bearing system; usually refers to the pack only.

ALMAR

Official message sent by HQMC to "All Marines" (Pronounced *all-mar*).

ALO

Air Liaison Officer; pilot who does a tour "slumming" with "Mud Marines."

ALPHAS
The Marine green uniform with blouse and ribbons.

Alpha Mike Foxtrot
Adios, Mother Fucker; goodbye; a polite form is "Adios My Friend."

Alpha Unit
A Marine's spouse.

Allotment
A specific amount of money deducted from a Marine's pay and sent to another entity.

AMC
Air Mobility Command; formerly known as the "Military Airlift Command"; see "MAC Flight."

AMF
See "Alpha Mike Foxtrot."

Ammo
Ammunition.

Amtrac
Slang for Amphibious Armored, Tracked, Personnel Carrier; also called an "LVT" or "AAV."

Amtracker
Assault Amphibious Vehicle crewman; also known as a "Tractor Rat."

Ammunition Supply Point (ASP)

Location just behind the FEBA where line units receive their ammunition resupply; also the location aboard a base where all ammo is stored while in garrison; in movies, an ASP is usually called an "ammo dump."

Anchor Clanker

Anyone in the Navy.

Anchor Pool

A betting pool; the winner is the one who comes closest to the time logged by the Officer of the Deck for dropping or weighing anchor.

Angel

KIA being transported; first used during OIF.

Angels

Altitude; measured in thousands of feet; "angels fifteen" means 15,000 feet above sea level.

ANGLICO

Air Naval Gunfire Liaison Company; composed of 4-man "fire control teams" used to direct NGF and CAS for allied nation forces or sister services; rarely work with Marine Corps units; members are usually parachute qualified to enable their deployment with Army Airborne units.

Ant Hill

Outpost with major communications assets; identified by large number of antennae ("ants") in the vicinity; also "Ant Farm."

Arc Light
B-52 bombers dropping their entire load of 2,000 pound bombs on suspected concentrations of enemy troops.

ARG
Amphibious Ready Group; consists of a Navy element - a group of ships known as an amphibious task force (ATF) - and a landing force (LF) of Marines.

Arlington Ridge
Location in Arlington VA north of the National Cemetery and overlooking the Potomac River; site of the Marine Corps War Memorial.

Arty
Artillery.

ARA
Aerial Rocket Artillery.

ARVN
Army of the Republic of Vietnam (Pronounced *r-vin*).

As You Were
Informal command to continue what you were doing; also used to indicate a correction to a previous order or comment.

ASAP
Literally means, "As Soon As Possible"; in actual fact it means, "Right now!" (Pronounced *a-sap*)

Asiatic
> Someone who has adopted local customs is said to have "gone Asiatic"; originally applied to members of the 4th Marine Regiment, the "China Marines."

ASP
> Ammunition Supply Point.

Assault Line
> Marine attack formation, with troops advancing abreast.

Ass Hanging Out
> Applied to someone who is either not squared away, or whose ignorance is showing.

Asshole to Bellybutton
> Troops (normally recruits) standing close together in line.

Assholes and Elbows
> To move quickly; i.e. "All I want to see is assholes and elbows!"

Assmosis
> Process by which some individuals get promoted; involves some serious "Ass Kissing."

Ass Pack
> A small pack worn on web gear, and located in the middle of the lower back; also called a "Butt Pack."

ASVAB
Armed Services Vocational Aptitude Battery; skills classification test required to join the armed forces (Pronounced *as-vab*).

At Ease
A command to troops in formation; "At ease" is a position of "rest" which allows free movement, although one foot must be kept in place and no talking is permitted; often used in other settings to tell someone to "be quiet!"

AWOL
Absent Without Leave; this term is NOT used by Marines (except in the movies); the proper term is "UA."

AWS
Amphibious Warfare School; attended by captains.

Aye
Yes; naval expression (Pronounced *eye*).

Aye Aye
I understand your order and will comply; naval expression (Pronounced *eye-eye*).

Azimuth
Compass heading.

Salty Language

Bravo

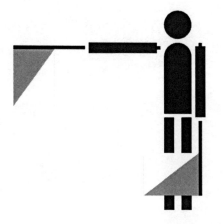

Salty Language

B1RD
Humorous identification for a non-existent Air Force plane. See "GU11." (Pronounced *b-one-r-d*).

BA-1100
Battery resembling a D-cell; used in the old starlight scopes; its existence lends credibility to the following humorous entry.

BA1100N
Fictional battery "FNGs" are sent in search of (Pronounced *b-a-eleven-hundred-november*); actually a *Balloon*.

BA-30
Government issue green Ray-o-vac "D" cell battery.

Ba Mu'o'i Ba
Brand name of a Vietnamese beer.

Baby Dicks
Small hot dogs contained in MREs.

Bad Conduct Discharge
Discharge ranking between Honorable and Dishonorable; also called a "Big Chicken Dinner" or "BCD."

Bag
To "get," as in, "to bag some sleep."

Bag Nasty
Meal delivered in a paper bag, mostly during Marksmanship Training at boot camp, but also at other times in the fleet; the reference is to the quality of the food contained in the bag.

Ball Bearing BAM
Male admin clerk.

BAM
A pejorative term for a Woman Marine; means "Broad Assed Marine"; Women Marines insist it actually means "Beautiful American Marine."

Banana Wars
Operations conducted by the Marine Corps in Haiti and Nicaragua between 1915 and 1934.

Bandit
Hostile aircraft; a "Bogey" which has been positively identified as a bad guy.

Bandoleer
Cloth or canvas bag containing of several *clips* of ammunition.

Bandolier
Linked belt of machinegun ammo.

BAQ
Basic Allowance for Quarters.

BAR
Browning Automatic Rifle; M1918A1 automatic rifle used from World War II until Vietnam; eventually replaced by the "SAW."

Bar Fine
Amount of money paid by bar girls in Subic Bay (in the Philippines) in order to be allowed to leave their bar or walk the streets; often paid by Americans who want to take the girls home.

Barnett, George

Twelfth Commandant of the Marine Corps; first graduate of the U. S. Naval Academy to be appointed Commandant; served as Major General Commandant from February 25, 1914 until June 30, 1920.

Barracks

Buildings where single Marines live; also a type of duty station (Marine Barracks) where Marines serve.

Barracks Cover

Frame cap with a leather bill, and a metal hoop frame for the cloth covering; it has a chin strap, which is usually worn above the bill; it is adorned with a large eagle, globe and anchor.

Barracks Rat

A Marine who does not go out on liberty much; also a woman who hangs around a barracks, BEQ or BOQ for the purpose of meeting Marines and/or giving or selling sexual favors.

Barrow, Robert H.

Twenty-seventh Commandant of the Marine Corps; served from July 1, 1979 until June 30, 1983.

Barstow

MCLB located in Barstow CA.

BAS

Basic Allowance for Subsistence; money paid in lieu of using military dining facilities; also called "ComRats."

Base Pay

Amount a service member earns per month based on rank and years of service.

Base Liberty

Liberty which is restricted to the confines of a base; also term used to describe a formation which has gotten loud or unruly, i.e. "I gave you at ease, not base liberty!"

Basic School

Where new second lieutenants are trained; conducted at Quantico, VA; see "TBS."

Basket Leave

An extended leave of absence from duty (beyond a 96 for example) which ends up not being charged as leave; often leave papers are actually filled out and approved, in order to cover everybody's ass in case the leave-taker gets arrested, killed or detained somehow while on leave; they remained in someone's "In Basket" (thus the term "basket leave") until the leave-taker returned; the papers are then destroyed and the leave is never recorded; an illegal way for a CO to reward someone, or for the company clerk to do his buddy a favor.

Basketball Ship

Flare ship (aircraft) on station to drop illumination flares on command; also called "Spooky."

Baton

Carried by a Drum Major; *not* the same as "swagger stick."

Battalion

Unit containing multiple companies; typically commanded by a lieutenant colonel; infantry and artillery battalions are normally assigned to a regiment.

Battalion Aid Station (BAS)

Field medical unit; the first organized aid station a Marine will see when transported from the care of the front line corpsmen; known as "Sick Bay" while in garrison.

Battle Dressing

A rectangular medical dressing carried into battle by each Marine.

Battle Jacket

Service green uniform jacket with a faux belt and no skirt used from World War II until the mid-1960s; see "Ike Jacket."

Battle Pin

Necktie clip; see also "Battle Scarf."

Battle Stations

See "General Quarters."

Battle Streamers

Streamers attached to a unit's "Colors" commemorating battles and campaigns participated in by that command, as well as the unit awards it has received.

Battery

Artillery unit equivalent to an infantry company; usually six guns; used in support of an infantry battalion.

Bayonet

(*n*) knife-like weapon attached to the muzzle of a rifle used for hand-to-hand combat. (*v*) the act of thrusting a bayonet into an enemy combatant.

Bazooka

A WWII period invention, it was the first of the modern rocket launched weapons and was made in 2.75" and 3.5" versions; used against tanks, vehicles and other hardened targets; replaced by the M72 "LAAW."

B-Billet

Independent Duty; a tour of duty as a "Drill Instructor," "Recruiter," or "Marine Security Guard (MSG)"; serving in one or more of these billets is important if a Marine wants to be competitive for promotion in the SNCO ranks (although they are not mandatory).

BB Stacker

Anyone dealing directly with ordnance.

BC Glasses

Birth Control Glasses; Marine Corps issue eyeglasses, so named by the troops due to their repulsive effect on the opposite sex; also "BCGs."

BCD

Bad Conduct Discharge.

B.C.G.s

See "B.C. Glasses"

BDA

Bomb Damage Assessment; determination of the effect of air attacks on a target; what every "Zoomie" flying "CAS" wants to know!

BDU

Battle Dress Uniform; the official name for cammies; used by the Army.

Beating a Dead Horse

A naval term meaning to work off advance pay aboard ship; the period before you start earning money again; see "Dead Horse."

Beef, Grease, and Shrapnel

C-Ration meal of Beefsteak, Potatoes and Gravy.

Beef and Rocks

C-Ration meal of Beef and Potatoes.

Belay

Stop; make fast; from the Naval practice of tying off a line; also "disregard," as in "Belay my last."

Belleau Wood

Legendary battle during WWI where Marines earned the nickname "Teufelhunden" (Devil Dogs) from the Germans; the French renamed the site of the battle "Bois de la Brigade de Marine" (Wood of the Marines) in honor of the Marines' valor.

Bellhop

See "Seagoing Bellhop."

Bells
> System of time on board ship; the routine day was broken into six watches of four-hours each. The watch on duty was responsible for maintaining the time so each half hour a bell would be rung beginning at thirty minutes into the watch with one bell, and ending up at the end of the watch with eight bells. Watches began at 12, 4 and 8 so that at those times eight bells were struck.

Below
> Downstairs; as in, "Go below."

Below Decks
> Decks below the main weather deck of a ship; they are numbered beginning with the main weather deck, which is 1; deck 7 is therefore seven decks below the main deck.

Bends and Thrusts
> Favorite "incentive PT" exercise of Drill Instructors; called "squat thrusts" by civilians and soldiers; also known as "Bends and Motherfuckers" or "Bends and Whoopies."

Bennie
> Shortened form of "benefit"; all services provided to or for soldiers, sailors, airmen or Marines are considered bennies.

BEQ
> Bachelor Enlisted Quarters (barracks).

Bestwick, Wilbur
First Sergeant Major of the Marine Corps; served from May 23, 1957 until Aug 31, 1959.

Betel nut
Narcotic seed nut chewed by Vietnamese villagers which turns their teeth and gums blood red.

Biddle, William
Eleventh Commandant of the Marine Corps; served as Acting Commandant in the rank of Colonel from Dec. 1, 1910 until Feb. 2, 1911, when he was appointed Major General Commandant; served until Feb. 12, 1914; during his tenure the term of office was set by law at four years.

Big Chicken Dinner
Bad Conduct Discharge.

Big Green Weenie
See "Green Weenie."

Big Nasty
See "Bag Nasty."

Bilge
Acrid mix of sea water, petroleum products and other brackish material which settles to the bottom of a ship; also information which is of no value; garbage; fail at something.

Bilge Rat
Sailors who drain and maintain the bilge on ship, or a Marine assigned to bilge duty as a form of punishment.

Billet
A specific job authorized within a unit structure.

Bingo
In Naval and Marine Aviation, a fuel level or condition requiring return to base, ship, or aerial refueler.

Binjo Ditch
Rudimentary sewage ditches found throughout Asia.

Bird
Aircraft; also a shortened version of "Shitbird."

Bird Colonel
Full colonel; pay grade O-6.

Bird Farm
Aircraft carrier.

Bird, Ball and Chain
Eagle, Globe and Anchor (usually used by short-timers).

Bird, Ball and Hook
A disrespectful reference to the modern emblem of the Marine Corps - the eagle, globe and anchor.

Birdmen
A pejorative term for airmen.

Bitchbox
The 1-MC used aboard ship; any amplified system used to pass information.

Bladensburg Pike
Location of the Marine line of defense on the edge of Washington D.C. when the British attacked during the War of 1812; the Marines were overrun by superior forces, but earned the respect of their enemy; some say the British spared the Commandant's House at 8th and I Streets SE as a result.

Black, Henry H.
Seventh Sergeant Major of the Marine Corps; served from June 1, 1975 until March 31, 1977.

Black Ace
A pilot who has crashed or lost five friendly aircraft.

Blanket Party
Used to "encourage" a screw-up to mend his ways. While he is sleeping his platoon-mates sneak up, cover him with a blanket, and administer numerous blows; not authorized, and punishable under the UCMJ; not often used; a good example took place in the movie "Full Metal Jacket."

Blister
Anything overstuffed; a rubber fuel bladder.

Blivet
Another form of "Blister."

Block
To tighten or straighten a field scarf (necktie).

Blood Chit
Notice carried by pilots and aircrew; displays messages aimed at civilians, asking them to help the pilot in the event he is shot down.

Blood Groove
Groove in a fighting knife or sword which allows blood to flow from a wound; as a result the blade can be removed more easily (a significant concern in close combat).

Blood Stripe
Red stripe worn down the outside of trouser legs on dress blue uniforms; worn by noncommissioned officers, warrant officers and commissioned officers; honors the high number of casualties among those ranks at the Battle of Chapultapec during the Mexican War.

Blood Wings
The gold "Navy/Marine Corps Parachutist Insignia" after it has been pounded into an awardee's chest several times; a rite of passage; see "Gold Wing Ceremony."

Bloop or Bloop 'em
Unofficial field command to hit a target with an M79 (or M-203) grenade launcher.

Blooper
M79 grenade launcher; at least one was assigned to each squad of infantry Marines in Vietnam; replaced by the M-203, which is attached to the M-16 rifle.

Blouse
The service or dress coat worn by Marines; also the act of tucking one's utility trouser legs into boots so that the fabric "bloused" over them; also the art of tucking in a shirt with military creases so that it appears tight over the entire belt line.

Blousing Bands
Elastic bands used for blousing utility trousers.

Blowing Smoke
Wasting time; talking for no purpose, and to no effect.

Blown Away
Killed.

BLT
Battalion Landing Team; the main body of infantrymen which make up a "MEU."

Blue Blood
Former enlisted Marine who crossed over and accepted a commission; see "Mustang."

Blue Falcon
Buddy Fucker; someone who screws you over.

Blue Nose
Someone who has crossed above the Arctic Circle while aboard ship, and has gone through the initiation; see "Line Crossing Ceremony."

Blue Peter
International Signal Flag for the letter "P"; it is a blue square with a white square within it; means all hands are to return to ship because it is preparing to go to sea.

Blues
The "Dress Blue" uniform.

Boat
Any small vessel incapable of making regular independent voyages on the high seas; also a submarine.

Boat Space
Slot for reenlistment within a given MOS; if there are more applicants than "Boat Spaces" the most qualified will be chosen until they are filled; from a term used to describe a "saved seat" aboard a small boat.

Body Armor
Modern version of the flak jacket; made of Kevlar.

Body Snatcher
Unit "Career Planner;" his job is to get you to reenlist!

Bogey
Unidentified object; usually an aircraft or ship.

BOHICA
Bend Over, Here It Comes Again; warning that you are about to get screwed (Pronounced *bow-hee-ka*).

Boiler Compound
Strong black coffee served aboard ship.

Boo-Coo
Many, or much; derived from the French "beaucoup."

Boondockers
Old version of the modern combat boot; shoes with high sides, manufactured to 1917 specifications; famous for having the heels come off; discontinued in the latter part of the 20th Century.

Boondocks
Any place out in the country; the middle of nowhere.

Boondoggle
Any situation in which the Marine gets more out of an assignment, job or situation than does the Marine Corps; a good time at the Uncle Sam's expense.

Boonies
Boondocks.

Boonie Hat
Field cover with a brim all the way around it; became an issue item in 2001 when the no-iron cammies were introduced; may not be worn in garrison; also "Bush Hat."

Boot
Recruit; rookie; newbie; someone who entered the military after you (even if it was only one day later!).

Boot Camp
Officially "Recruit Training"; conducted at the Marine Corps Recruit Depots at Parris Island S.C. and San Diego CA.

Boots and Utes
Uniform combination consisting of the utility uniform (the uniform worn in the field) and boots; most often proscribed for physical training events (Pronounced *boots-and-youts*).

BOQ
Bachelor Officer Quarters.

Boresight
Line up the axis of a weapon with its sights; commonly done with tanks; pilots also use the term to describe the act of concentrating on a small detail to the point of losing sight of "the big picture."

Bounce
Unexpected attack on another aircraft; i.e. "Pappy Boyington *bounced* a pair of Zeros."

Bouncing Betty
U.S. anti-personnel mine which pops into the air to waist level before exploding.

Box of Grid Squares
One of the endless group of nonexistent items new members of a unit are sent looking for; used mainly in artillery units.

Box Kicker
Marine who works in a "Supply MOS."

Boxsee
Vietnamese word for doctor; Marines called their corpsmen by this name.

Brain Bucket
Helmet of any type, including combat Kevlar and aviation headgear.

Brain Fart
Silly mistake; loss of concentration; a senior moment.

Brain Housing Group
Place where thought process takes place; human head; also "melon" or "grape."

Brass
Officers.

Brat
See "Military Brat."

Bravo Zulu
Well done; from the Allied Naval Signal Book (ACP-175 Series) adopted after the formation of NATO.

Break Out
Get out; i.e. "Break out your ID card."

Brevet Promotion
Temporary, often honorary, commissions enabling the owner to wear the uniform and collect the pay of that rank while yet being listed in the official lists with a lower rank.

Bridge
Compartment from which a ship is controlled while at sea.

Brig
A jail in the naval services; usually operated by Marines.

Brig Chaser
A Marine (now normally an MP) assigned to guard a prisoner while he is being transported to a location outside the brig, often for a work detail; also "Chaser."

Brig Rat
Prisoner; someone who is frequently in trouble.

Brig Step
A regular step as in marching, but the distance between one prisoner and the back of the one to his front is reduced to about four inches so that they must all step together; common method of controlling prisoners while moving them from place to place; illegal step for anyone other than a prisoner.

Brigadier General
First of the Flag Officer ranks of commissioned officers; signified by a silver star on the collar or epaulet of the uniform; pay grade is O-7.

Bronze Star
Personal decoration originally intended for valorous service; by the end of the 20th Century it was being given out for many non-combat acts; sometimes known as the "officers' good conduct medal"; the value of the award became so deflated a metal "V" device is now worn on the suspension ribbon to indicate valor.

Brown Nose
Kiss Ass.

Brown Shoe Marine
An old salt; until Secretary of Defense MacNamara forced all of the services to use the same shoes, Marines were issued brown shoes; in the early 1960s the shoe color changed to black, but old salts continued to wear their brown shoes as long as they could get away with it.

Brown Side Out

Helmet covers and shelter halves were once green camouflage on one side, and brown camouflage on the other; this was the instruction to place the brown on the outside; often used to describe confusion in orders, as the color would change frequently and ultimately someone would show up for formation with the wrong color showing.

Brownbagger

Someone who lives off base; person who carries lunch rather than eat at the mess hall; usually a married Marine.

Bucket of Steam

A commodity used in a practical joke by "salty" Marines, who would send inexperienced boots on a mission to find one.

Buckle

Fight furiously; as in, "Buckle for your dust."

Bubble

SCUBA pin worn by military divers.

Bucket

Woman Marines' version of a "Barracks Cover."

Buddy

Friend; the old joke is a *real* buddy is someone who will go into town when you are restricted to base and get himself two blow jobs, and then come back and give one of them to *you*.

Salty Language

Buddy Unit
> Two Marines, usually half a fire team; emerging as the basic urban combat fighting unit.

Bug Juice
> Colored, sweetened water served aboard ship or in mess halls; military "Kool-Aid"; also bug repellant.

Bug Out
> To leave quickly, usually as a unit; an individual would "bug."

Bulkhead
> Wall; from the naval term for a water-tight structure between compartments on a ship.

Bull
> The center or highest scoring part of a target; often called a "Bull's Eye."

Bullshit
> Card game played by groups of Marines while standing in line, usually aboard ship. A player will draw five cards from a shuffled deck and after reviewing the hand will announce the hand (it can be anything from "One Jack" to "Full Boat, Flush"). The next Marine in line will decide if the announced hand is what the player has, and will either accept or proclaim "bullshit." If the hand is accepted the Marine can draw from one to five cards and announce the hand, but this hand must be better than the hand he accepted. This continues until someone calls "bullshit"; there is no scoring.

Bum Scoop
Bad information; often passed on by "Bum Scoop Ned."

Bumfucknowhere.
The middle of nowhere; also "Bumfuck Egypt."

Bunker
A covered and reinforced fighting hole.

Burrows, William Ward
Second Marine Commandant; promoted to Lieutenant Colonel Commandant on May 1, 1800; died in office on March 6, 1804.

Bush
Outside the perimeter wire; the boonies.

Bust
Reduce in rank.

Bust Caps
Engage in a firefight; fire a weapon.

Bust Heavies
Work hard.

Butler, Smedley
The only officer ever awarded two Medals of Honor; known as "Old Gimlet Eye."

Butts
Target pits on a rifle range.

Butt Kit
Ash tray; often a #10 tin can filled with dirt or sand.

Butter Bar
Second lieutenant or ensign; from the gold color of their rank insignia; also "Brown Bar."

Bursting Bomb
Insignia used in the Marine Corps to designate a warrant officer with an MOS which entitles him to be called "gunner"; also used on the enlisted grade insignia of master gunnery sergeant.

Butt Pack
See "Ass Pack."

Buy The Farm
Get killed.

Buzzard, Ball and Hook
Another version of "Bird, Ball and Chain."

By the Numbers
In sequence; from the beginning; used to indicate an action which must be done precisely as directed.

By your leave...
Phrase spoken by a junior when overcoming a senior prior to passing; also a request to be allowed to depart; usually followed by "sir" or 'ma'am."

Charlie

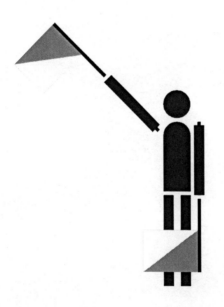

Salty Language

C-4

Plastic explosive.

C-Rations

Individual meals used in the field from World War II through Vietnam; they came in a box containing cans of food and a foil accessory pack; replaced by the "MRE."

Cactus Air Force

Rag-tag group of Marine fighter planes who flew out of Henderson Field on Guadalcanal during the early days of WWII against overwhelming odds; derived from the code name for Guadalcanal, which was "Cactus."

Cadence

Used by a unit leader marching troops in formation to keep then in step; can be intricate, or as simple as "left, right, left, right"; also the practice of singing (by an entire unit) during a formation PT run.

Cadillacs

Boots; the predominant form of transportation for recruits and infantry Marines; also "Leather Personnel Carriers."

Cake Hole

Mouth; also "Pie Hole" or "Soup Cooler."

Call Sign

Word identifier for a unit, aircraft or pilot on the radio.

CamelBac®
Name brand version of a personal hydration system which allows the wearer to sip water through a tube from a bladder worn on his back.

Cammies
Field uniform of the Marine Corps since the 1970s; in 2002 the "digital" design was introduced. The design itself includes tiny Marine Corps emblems, and blends better into most natural settings.

Camp Butler
MCB located in Hawaii; home of much of the 3rd Marine Division; actually a series of camps located throughout the island; named after Smedley Darlington Butler.

Camp Lejeune
MCB located in eastern North Carolina; home of the 2nd Marine Division; named for John A. Lejeune.

Camp Pendleton
MCB located in southern California; home of the 1st Marine Division; named for Joseph H. Pendleton.

Camp Smith
MCB in Hawaii; home of the 1st Marine Brigade; named for General Holland M. "Howlin' Mad" Smith.

Campaign Cover
Hat worn by drill instructors; only official Marine headgear not always called a cover; also called a "Smokey Bear."

Canine and Equestrian Theater
See "Dog and Pony Show."

Cannon Cocker
Marine in the artillery; also "Gun Bunny."

Canoe U
The U.S. Naval Academy at Annapolis.

CACO
Casualty Assistance Calls Officer; often part of an I&I Staff; visits families of Marines to make notification of death or injury; the Marine Corps does not, and never has, make such notifications by telegram as other services have done; this is easily the most difficult job in the Corps; sometimes called a "CAO" (Pronounced *cack-oh*)

CAP
Combat Air Patrol; also a "Combined Action Platoon," which was a unit of Marines and Vietnamese soldiers working together as part of a "Pacification Program."

Cap
To fire at something or someone; from the act of busting the primer cap on a round of ammunition; see "Busting Caps."

Captain
Third grade of commissioned officer; most senior of the company grade officers; indicated by two silver bars on the collar or epaulet of the uniform; the rank

insignia for a Captain of Marines differs from every other service's O-3 rank insignia (the tie-bars are at the ends of the rank bars instead of somewhat inboard); pay grade is O-3; not to be confused with a Navy captain, whose pay grade is O-6.

Captain's Mast
Non-judicial punishment exercised by a ship's captain.

CAR
Combat Action Ribbon; personal decoration of the Navy and Marine Corps; awarded to those who are at or below the rank of Colonel (O-6) and actively participate in ground or surface combat.

Career Planner
A unit's "recruiter"; his job is to find qualified, quality Marines who want to "Ship Over" for another "Cruise"; also known as the "Career Jammer" or "Body Snatcher."

Carry On
Informal order to continue what you were doing before being interrupted by the appearance of a commissioned officer.

CAS
Close Air Support.

Casual Company (or Platoon)
Unit composed exclusively of Marines awaiting reassignment or discharge.

Casualty Call
See "CACO."

Cat
Catapult; device on an aircraft carrier which hurls aircraft into the air; operated by a giant steam piston.

Cat 4
Applicants who score next to the lowest on military entrance exams; under normal circumstances they would not be allowed to enlist, but during times of war and when recruiting was difficult, a number have been allowed to join; in 1960 the Pentagon was forced to accept some social engineering called "Project 100,000" (aka "McNamara's 100,000") in which a great number of Cat 4 enlistees were taken in - and the military has yet to recover; for classification purposes the category was further broken down into 4a, 4b or 4c, defined by recruiters as "animal," "vegetable," or "mineral."

Cat 9
A reference to someone who is "*beyond* dumb," since Category 4 is the lowest of scores on the entrance exams.

Cates, Clifton B.
Nineteenth Commandant of the Marine Corps; served as Commandant from Jan 1, 1948 until Dec 31, 1951 in the rank of General.

CATF
Commander Amphibious Task Force; usually an Admiral, the CATF retains control over the Landing Force until Marines have established a beachhead

ashore, at which time it is handed off to the CLF (pronounced *cat-if*)

Cattle Car
Cargo trailer converted to the purpose of carrying troops by adding bus doors to the right side, sealing the back doors, and adding bench seating; *extremely* uncomfortable.

CC
Correctional Custody; where disciplinary problems are sent to become "enlightened"; akin to a chain gang.

CAX
Combined Arms Exercise; live-fire exercise for a MAGTF.

CG
Commanding General.

CH-46 Sea Knight
Twin-engine helicopter capable of carrying a platoon of Marines; older than most *Marines*.

Chain of Command
The continuous chain of authority which links the most junior private to the Commander-in-Chief, and vice versa. Many argue that the U. S. implementation of the chain of command is the most important strategy employed by our military forces. In other armies the loss of a commander would throw the entire organization into disorder, while in the U. S.

military the next most senior person present simply assumes command; it is taught that whenever two Marines are walking together, *one* is in charge.

Chairman of the Joint Chiefs of Staff

General or admiral appointed by the President to serve as his senior military advisor; works with the Secretary of Defense; has no direct authority over the individual services; does, however, direct the Unified Commands; General Peter Pace became the first Marine CJCS in 2005.

Challenge

A word or phrase given by a sentry to someone who is approaching his post; the approaching person must then give the correct password, otherwise the sentry will assume he is an enemy or unauthorized person.

Challenge Coin

Coin shared by members of a specific organization; used to informally identify a member of that group.

CHAMPUS

Civilian Health And Medical Program of the Uniformed Services; military HMO; now called "TRICARE."

Chaplain

Religious leader commissioned into the Navy to provide religious services to and for members of the Naval establishment; addressed as "Chaplain" regardless of rank; also called a "Sky Pilot" (but not to their face).

Chapman Jr., Leonard F.
Twenty-fourth Commandant of the Marine Corps; served from Jan. 1, 1968 until Dec. 31, 1971.

Charlie
Vietnamese Communist soldier; abbreviated "VC" or "Victor Charlie," thus "Charlie"; also "Mr. Charles."

Charlie Foxtrot
Phonetic version of "Cluster Fuck."

Charlie Sierra
Chicken Shit.

Check
Yes; affirmative; I agree.

Check Your Six
Look behind you; from aviation term, "6 o'clock" referring to the relative location of an aircraft, with 12 o'clock being to the front of the airplane; also "Watch your six."

Chem Light
Common term for Cyalume chemical glow sticks.

Cherry Boy
Newcomer to the Orient; male virgin.

Cherry Jump
First parachute jump with parent unit after completing airborne training; cherry jumpers are considered to be dangerous, and are required to wear a specially painted helmet announcing them as such.

Cherry Point
MCAS in eastern North Carolina; home of the 2nd Marine Air Wing.

Chesty
Lieutenant General Lewis B. "Chesty" Puller, the most legendary Marine who ever lived; many Drill Instructors require their recruits to recite, "Good night Chesty, wherever you are!" upon retiring at night.

Chevron
Basic element of the enlisted rank structure; until the late 19th Century chevrons were worn in the European tradition, with the point facing down; today the normal position for a chevron in the United States military is with the point up (except in the Navy).

Chi-Com
Chinese Communist; also a "Chinese Communist grenade."

Chicken Shit
Stupid and petty stuff, usually directed by someone of more rank and/or authority.

Chief
Navy Chief Petty Officer.

Chief's Mess
Where Chiefs (and embarked Marine SNCOs) eat and relax aboard ship; they have the best chow in the Navy, which is probably one reason why Chiefs tend to be a bit on the, shall we say, "portly" side.

Chief of Naval Operations
Abbreviated CNO; highest ranking Naval Officer; reports to the Secretary of the Navy; sits as a regular member of the Joint Chiefs of Staff; eligible to serve as Chairman; holds the rank of admiral; the Commandant of the Marine Corps does *not* report to the CNO.

Chief Warrant Officer
Warrant Officer who has been commissioned; the top four grades of Warrant Officer (W-2 through W-5) are commissioned officers (W-1s are *appointed*).

Chieu-Hoi
Unconditional surrender by an enemy soldier or force in Vietnam; "chieu-hoi chits" offered them amnesty.

China Marines
Marines of the 4th Marine Regiment assigned to China in the first half of the 20th Century; also called "Horse Marines."

Chit
Any piece of paper authorizing something (light duty chit, leave chit, etc.)

Chop Chop
Quickly; in a hurry; derived from Chinese by the old China Marines.

Chopper
Helicopter; term is usually used by the Army; Marines and sailors call them "helos."

Chosin Reservoir
Fiercest and most costly battle in the Korean War; legendary withdrawal under fire in freezing temperatures against a well-trained, much larger force.

Chow Hall
Place where meals are served; sometimes called "Mess Hall" or "Dining Facility"; see "Mess Deck."

Church Key
Can opener.

CID
Criminal Investigation Division; unit of Military Police charged with criminal investigations, polygraph examinations and other detective work; wear civilian clothing; rank is indicated as "Investigator."

CINC
Commander-In-Chief.

CINC House
A Marine's spouse (usually a wife); also "Alpha Unit."

Cinderella Liberty
Liberty which expires at midnight; used mostly in foreign ports where the ship's captain is concerned for the safety of his crew, or as a subliminal form of punishment.

CIT
Counter Intelligence Team; unit with the mission of thwarting enemy attempts to gather intelligence.

CivDiv

See "1ˢᵗ CivDiv."

Civvies

Civilian clothing.

Class VI

Military liquor store; from the priority level assigned to the shipment of such supplies during World War II; often written "Class 6."

Class A

The green service uniform with ribbons; used until about 1980; replaced by the term "Alphas."

Claymore.

Directional anti-personnel mine; uses plastic explosives to propel ball bearings; used in ambushes and perimeter defense.

Cleary, Robert E.

Tenth Sergeant Major of the Marine Corps; served from June 28, 1983 until June 26, 1987.

CLF

Commander Landing Force; senior Marine in charge of the ground forces involved in an amphibious landing; assumes overall control from the CATF once a beachhead has been established (pronounced *clef* or *cliff*).

Click

Inexact distance derived from artillery sightings in which each click of site elevation would move the impact point depending on a number of diverse options; usually means a kilometer.

Clip

Device used to issue several rounds of ammunition at one time; a clip of 5.56 mm 'M-16 ammo' holds 10 rounds, and there are 14 clips to a bandoleer; *not* to be confused with a "Magazine," which is what a Marine fills with ammo and inserts into his weapon.

Close Air Support (CAS)

Concept developed by the Marine Corps during the "Banana Wars" of the 1930s and copied by the Germans in World War II; used to attack enemy positions or formations only yards from Marine front lines; Marine aviators are most proficient at it, but flying sailors also do an acceptable job; the Navy calls it, "Moving mud to help out the grunts"; A good example can be found in the John Wayne movie "Flying Leathernecks."

Close Order Drill (COD)

Method of moving Marines from point A to point B in an orderly fashion; the practice also instills discipline, and promotes instantaneous obedience to orders; what civilians call "Marching"; all Marines are good at it, but the "Silent Drill Platoon" takes it to the level of fine art.

Cluster Fuck

A mission, operation or activity gone bad; confusion; also "Gaggle Fuck."

Circle Jerk

See "Cluster Fuck."

CLNC
Camp Lejeune, North Carolina.

CMC
Commandant of the Marine Corps; senior officer in the Marine Corps, although under the Joint Chiefs of Staff and Unified Command systems of organization it is possible to have a Marine whose billet outranks the Commandant (General Peter Pace, Chairman of the Joint Chiefs of Staff, is in a position which outranks the Commandant).

CN
See "CS."

CO
Commanding Officer; also a "Conscientious Objector."

Coastie
Member of the Coast Guard.

Coaxial Machinegun
Machinegun mounted exactly alongside a tank's cannon, enabling the tank's gunner to use the same fire control system for both weapons; also "Coax."

Cobra
AH-1 Sea Cobra attack helicopter; often called a "Snake."

COC
Combat Operations Center; sometimes called the "Center of Confusion."

Cock Holster
See "Dick Holster."

COD
Close Order Drill.

Code Talkers
Navajo Marines who were recruited during World War II to serve as field radio operators; they would translate messages into a code based upon the Navajo language and transmit them to another Code Talker, who would then translate it back into English; the only field code never broken by the Japanese.

Colonel
Sixth grade of commissioned officer; senior field grade officer; indicated by a silver eagle (always facing forward) on the collar of the uniform; pay grade is O-6; sometimes called a "Full" or "Bird" Colonel.

Colors
Time of day when the national flag is hoisted or lowered from the flagpole; all personnel stop and render appropriate honors during this period; also the flag of a specific unit upon which battle streamers are mounted.

Color Guard
Detail consisting of right and left guards armed with rifles, an American flag bearer, and a bearer for the Marine Corps or unit "Colors."

Color Sergeant of the Marine Corps
By regulation, the most senior sergeant (E-5) in the Marine Corps; assigned to Marine Barracks 8th and I; has charge of the official Battle Colors of the Marine Corps.

Combat Town
Nickname given to "MOUT" facilities; see "MOUT."

Commandant's Own
The United States Marine Corps Drum and Bugle Corps.

Combat Correspondents
Marines who report war news from the front and assist the news media in reporting about Marines in combat; trained at the Defense Information School.

Commandant of the Marine Corps (CMC)
The highest ranking member of the Marine Corps; the first CMC was a captain, and the rank has increased until today he holds the rank of general; appointed by the President; reports to the Secretary of the Navy; sits as a regular member of the Joint Chiefs of Staff, and eligible to serve as Chairman.

Commander in Chief (CINC)
The President of the United States.

Commanding General (CG)
General officer in charge of a unit with authorities granted under the UCMJ to dispense justice commensurate with his rank.

Commanding Officer (CO)
Officer in charge of a unit with authorities granted under the UCMJ to dispense justice commensurate with his rank.

Commando
Not wearing skivvies.

Command Voice
The voice used while drilling troops; characterized by distinctness, volume, inflection, and projection.

Commissary
Grocery store on base; run by DeCA (Defense Commissary Agency).

Commissioned Officer
Officers who have been designated "officers and gentlemen" by Congress on the advice of the President; noncommissioned officers are rated, and warrant officers are granted warrants to their grade; enlisted Marines are fond of noting that their *parents* made them gentlemen - it did *not* require an act of Congress!

Comm Wire
Field telephone wire, also called "Slash Wire."

Company
Unit containing more than one platoon; typically commanded by a captain; companies are assigned within battalions.

Company Grade
Commissioned officers in the first three grades: second lieutenant, first lieutenant and captain; traditionally in the naval services these officers may be addressed as "Mister," but this rarely occurs in the Marine Corps.

Company Gunny
Usually a gunnery sergeant in a company charged with training; a billet, not a rank.

Composite Score
Mathematical calculation used to measure certain Marines against each other within a given grade and MOS; computed quarterly for all lance corporals and corporals who are eligible for promotion to corporal and sergeant, respectively; used to determine whether or not a Marine will get promoted; arrived at using a formula which combines rifle range score, PFT score, Pro/Con marks, TIG, and TIS; see "Cutting Score."

ComRats
Commuted Rations; payment in lieu of eating in the mess hall; usually paid to married Marines; also called "BAS."

COMSEC
Communications Security; (*n*) equipment and software used to encrypt radio and other transmissions; (*v*) the act of ensuring such transmissions are secure.

Comshaw
See "Cumshaw."

Concertina
Heavy duty barbed wire; looks like a giant slinky.

CONEX Box
Large lockable metal box used to store and ship equipment; actually stands for "Container, Express."

Confederate States Marine Corps
Many officers of the CSM were formerly officers or noncommissioned officers in the U. S. Marine Corps before they resigned to "go south."

Confidence Course
A series of large-scale obstacles which a Marine must overcome, particularly in boot camp; generally not a timed event; most often an individual effort designed to overcome fear of height and develop confidence in recruits; different from the "Obstacle Course"; recruits can be seen on part of the Confidence Course in the movie "Full Metal Jacket."

Congressional Medal of Honor
There is NO SUCH THING; see "Medal of Honor."

CONGRINT
Congressional Investigation.

Conscientious Objector (CO)
Someone who objects to combat on (supposedly) religious grounds; can serve in non-combatant positions (including service on the battlefield as a corpsman or other unarmed person) or in non-military public service assignments. Some are legitimate, but others lie and use this designation as a means of self-preservation.

CONUS
Continental United States; the contiguous 48 states.

Cool Beans
Outstanding; everything is OK.

Cop
To "get," as in "cop some Zs."

Corfam®
Material used to make dress shoes and boots with a high gloss finish; shoes made of this material have come to be known as "Corfams."

Corp
Abbreviation for the word "corporation"; frequently used incorrectly in place of the word "Corps."

Corporal of Marines
First of the noncommissioned officer ranks; indicated by two chevrons with crossed rifles; worn on both collars or sleeves; pay grade is E-4.

Corps
Military unit containing multiple divisions, or a unique, specified military organization given the designation.

Corps and Country
Traditional final toast at "Mess Nights"; made with "1775 Rum Punch"; at the invitation of the Mess President, Mr. Vice says, "Long live the United States, and success to the Marines!"; *must* be "bottomed up."

Corpsman

Enlisted member of the Navy Medical Corps trained in field medical aid; during WWII they were called "Pharmacist Mates"; often wear Marine Corps uniforms with Navy rank and insignia; can be identified by a "Caduceus" worn on the left collar; usually called "Doc."

Cosmolene®

Protective fluid placed on rifles and other metal objects; hardens and keeps item from rusting or corroding; must be removed before item can be used; also refers to something new, as in "it was still in cosmolene."

Cookie Duster

Moustache.

Court Street

Liberty destination in Jacksonville N.C. for Marines from Camp Lejeune, Camp Geiger and MCAS New River; until the 1980s the street was populated with bars, pawn shops and the bus station; the town has since cleaned it up.

Cover

Caps, hats and other things worn on the head; Marines wear covers, *not* hats; a Marine's cover is *always* removed when indoors, unless that Marine is "under arms"; also, in ranks, to align directly behind the Marine in front of you.

Coxswain

Someone who steers a small boat (Pronounced *cox-sun*).

CP
Command Post; headquarters.

CP Tent
Small tent specially designed for use as a CP.

CPO
See "Chief."

Cracker Jacks
Jumpsuits worn by sailors; can also be the sailors themselves.

Crawford, Leland D.
Ninth Sergeant Major of the Marine Corps; served from Aug. 16, 1979 until June 27, 1983.

Crew-Served Weapon
Any weapon which requires more than one Marine to operate it; artillery pieces, mortars and large machine guns fit into this category.

Cross Deck
Transfer from one ship to another; sometimes done while underway.

Crossing the Line
Ceremony performed aboard a ship whenever it crosses a navigational line such as the equator or Arctic Circle; very colorful, and usually involves an initiation of those who have never crossed that particular line before; see "Shellback" and "Blue Nose."

Crotch, The
The Marine Corps (pejorative form); only a *Marine* is entitled to use this term – all others risk severe bodily harm; also see "Suck, The."

Crucible
54-hour training event in which Marine recruits are physically and mentally challenged by lack of sleep, minimal food, forced marches, teamwork exercises and leadership opportunities; the final major training event of boot camp; designed to pull together everything recruits have been taught previously; culminates in the "Warrior Breakfast."

Cruise
Period of enlistment; also a deployment aboard ship.

Crumb Catcher
Mouth.

CS
Non-lethal riot control agent; commonly called "tear gas" in the civilian world; can be deployed via grenades or cluster bombs; used to train Marines in proper NBC procedures, or to deny an enemy the use of an area; a milder, but longer lasting, form is called "CN."

Cumshaw
Present or gratuity; often a piece of needed equipment which appears when needed (while at the same time a *similar* item disappears from another unit); a cumshaw artist is generally prized within a unit for his ability to provide - and few questions are

asked; from the old Chinese term "kam sia" meaning "grateful thanks"; the term was originally used at the start of World War II to describe payoffs by Honolulu's Hotel Street prostitutes to local police officials; also "Comshaw."

Cunt Cap
Garrison cover for WMs; female version of "Pisscutter."

Cupola
Tank commander's hatch.

CUPP
Combined Unit Pacification Program; Vietnam era; similar to "CAP."

Cushman Jr., Robert E.
Twenty-fifth Commandant of the Marine Corps; served from Jan. 1, 1972 until June 30, 1975.

Cutting Score
Score periodically announced by HQMC for each MOS; it is the number to which individual composite scores are compared in to control the number of promotions to Corporal and Sergeant; if your "Composite Score" is equal to or higher than your "Cutting Score," you're in (provided you are recommended by your CO and otherwise qualified); see "Composite Score."

Delta

Salty Language

D

See "LSD."

Da Nang

Seaport on the South China Sea in southern "I Corps" in RVN; location of a major Marine Corps base.

Dailey, Joseph W.

Fifth Sergeant Major of the Marine Corps; served from Aug 1, 1969 until Jan 31, 1973.

Daily Seven

Basic "Physical Training" exercises.

Daly, Daniel J.

The only enlisted Marine to be awarded the Medal of Honor twice; famous for saying, "Come on you sons of bitches! Do you want to live forever?" at Belleau Wood.

Dark Green Marine

Black Marine; all Marines are *green*, just in different shades.

Dash Two

The second aircraft in a formation of two or more; the wingman; slang for a Marine pilot's spouse.

Data Dink

Marine who works with computers.

Date of Enlistment

For enlisted personnel; the third level used to

determine precedence among individuals of the same rank; the senior of two persons of the same rank is determined by the earliest date of rank; among two or more where rank and date of rank are identical, the one with the earliest date of enlistment is senior; the junior of the two is then jokingly referred to as a "boot"; officially called the "Pay Entry Base Date" (PEBD).

Date of Commissioning

For commissioned officers; serves the same purpose as Date of Enlistment does for enlisted personnel; seldom used, as precedence among officers is much more structured.

Date of Promotion

Date on which a promotion warrant or order is presented.

Date of Rank

Date on which a promotion is effective; it is usually prior to date of promotion (sometimes by days, sometimes weeks, sometimes years depending on the requirements of the promoting authority); used to establish precedence for promotion to the next higher rank, and establish seniority among individuals of the same rank.

DD Form 4

Enlistment contract; all promises made by recruiters *must* be listed on the Form 4 - or they are not real.

DD Form 214
Certificate of service issued upon discharge; lists all pertinent service information such as rank, date of rank, awards, special education and nature of service (honorable, bad conduct, dishonorable).

Deadline
Procedure which takes a piece of equipment off the operational rolls for repairs; sometimes used in reference to injured personnel.

Deck
Floor; from the naval term.

Deck Ape
Anyone in the Deck Force aboard ship (sailors who chip paint, swab decks, mend canvas and create ornamental rope work); generally a Boatswain's Mate.

Deep Six
To throw something overboard or away; shitcan; hide; originally the call of a sailor to the bridge that the depth of the water is more than six, but not quite seven, fathoms.

DEERS
Defense Enrollment Eligibility Reporting System (used to register dependents for CHAMPUS and numerous other programs).

Defilade
Cut or low spot in the ground used for cover by tanks and personnel.

Delayed Enlistment Program (DEP)

Recruiting procedure which allows a person to enlist in the inactive reserve prior to being ordered to active duty; legally binds the person to enlistment, and gives him or her seniority when ordered to active duty; see "Poolee."

Delta Sierra

Dumb Shit.

DEP

Delayed Enlistment Program.

Department of the Navy (DON)

The unit, under the Department of Defense, which manages the Navy and Marine Corps; there are also Departments of the Army and Air Force; sailors like to remind Marines that the Corps is part of the DON; Marines just reply "That's right, we're the *Men's* Department!"

Dependent

Usually the spouse and children of military people; others can be dependents if they meet dependency criteria.

Deployment

Leaving the normally assigned duty area, usually as a unit, to serve temporarily in another area; often aboard ship; see "Float."

DEROS

Date of Estimated Return from Overseas; when you are supposed to return to CONUS after a deployment.

Desertion
Unauthorized absence of more than 30 days.

Detachment Commander
SNCO in charge of an MSG detachment; this is the only "Command Billet" available to enlisted Marines; formerly called the NCOIC; members of the State Department tend to refer to this Marine as the "The Gunny" regardless of his rank, a practice which delights staff sergeants and ticks off master sergeants.

DetCmdr
Detachment Commander.

Deuce and a Half
Two and a half ton truck; also known as a "Six-By" (it has six wheel drive).

Deuce Gear
See "782 gear."

Devil Doc
Nickname for Navy hospital corpsmen assigned to Marine Corps field units.

Devil Dog
A Marine; translated from the name "Teufelhunden," which was given to the Marines by their German enemies in World War I.

Devil Dyke
Uncomplimentary nickname given to WMs; based on the theory many are lesbians; not widely used.

Devil Pup
Member of an organization designed to help boys and girls from all backgrounds gain self-confidence and learn to take responsibility for their actions; not a Marine Corps sponsored program; also a nickname sometimes given to the children of Marines.

De Weldon, Dr. Felix W.
Sculptor of the "Marine Corps War Memorial."

DI
Abbreviation for "Drill Instructor"; this term is routinely used by everyone but *recruits*.

Di Di
From the Vietnamese term "Di Di Mau" which loosely translates to "move quickly" or "run." (Pronounced *d-d*).

Dick Cheese
Someone of little of no value as a person; worthless as a member of a unit or team.

Dick Dance
See "Cluster Fuck."

Dick Holster
Mouth; usually used in reference to Women Marines; also "Cock Holster."

Dick Skinners
Hands.

Diddie Bop

To move in such a manner as to be extremely cool; move in a casual manner.

Dining In

Function similar to a "Mess Night" which *may* be attended by spouses and dates.

Dink

VC or, generically, Vietnamese.

Dinky Dau

Vietnamese term translated by Americans to mean "crazy."

Dinged

Wounded.

Ditty Dot

Radio operator; from Morse Code (dit and dot).

Division

Unit containing multiple (usually three) regiments plus supporting units; commanded by a major general.

Dixie Cup

Headgear worn by enlisted sailors through the grade of E-6 (first class petty officer); see "White Hat."

DMO

Diving Medical Officer; Navy doctor who specializes in diving medicine.

DMZ

Demilitarized Zone; in Vietnam, the section between the Marines of I Corps and North Vietnam; in Korea, the line drawn at the 38th Parallel; any buffer between two belligerent camps.

Doc

Term reserved for Navy enlisted hospital corpsmen assigned to duty with Marine Corps combat units; these sailors are generally given the same respect one Marine gives to another; Navy corpsmen who earn service medals during duty with the Marine Corps are authorized to wear a miniature eagle, globe and anchor on their ribbon - something not even authorized for Marines.

Doctor

Commissioned officer in the Navy with a degree in medicine, dentistry, psychology or other allied profession; usually referred to by their military rank.

Dogface

Soldier.

Dog and Pony Show

A presentation or display which is somewhat contrived or overly intricate; done to demonstrate equipment, techniques or capabilities; a more formal version is "Canine and Equestrian Theater."

Doggies

Soldiers.

Dog Robber
Aide to a general officer whose duties are so varied as to defy explanation.

Dogs
Feet.

Dog Tags
Metal disks embossed with personal information which can be left with a body on the field of battle for identification; see also "Toe Chain."

Donkey Dick
Long, flexible metal spout for attaching to "Jerry Cans."

Dope
Sight adjustments made to a rifle to make its firing more accurate; usually used in reference to marksmanship training or qualification; also any adjustment made to improve the outcome of any event.

Dope on a Rope
Static-line parachuting.

Double Digit Midget
A "short-timer" with less than 100 days remaining on his enlistment or overseas tour; sometimes called a "Two Digit Midget."

Double Time
Marching pace double that of "quick time" in which the arms are bent at the elbow and the troops run in step.

Dragon
Type of man-packed, wire-guided anti-tank weapon.

Dragon Wagon
See "LVS."

Dress Blues
The famous blue uniform of Marines with a standing collar; similar to those worn by Marines during the Civil War.

Dress Blue A
Full Dress Blues with medals; worn on special occasions; not authorized for liberty.

Dress Blue B
Full Dress Blues with ribbons and badges.

Dress Blue C
Blue trousers, khaki shirt, field scarf and ribbons; usually worn in assignments such as recruiting.

Dress Blue D
Blue trousers, short sleeve khaki shirt and ribbons; usually worn in assignments such as recruiting.

Dress Blues, Shower Shoes, and a Light Coat of Oil
Flip response to the question, "what is the uniform" or "what will you be wearing."

Drill
Training period for reservists; usually one weekend per month; also the act of conducting "COD."

Drill Field
Where a Drill Instructor plies his trade; often called "The Street" amongst DIs.

Drill Instructor
Noncommissioned officer charged with the training of Marine recruits and the making of Marines; each recruit platoon usually has three drill instructors: a senior drill instructor and two junior drill instructors.

Drill Instructor's Hut
Office and duty quarters of drill instructors; located within the recruit squad bay.

Drill Sergeant
Army recruit instructor, *never* to be confused with a Marine Drill Instructor; the first batch of modern Army Drill Sergeants were trained at the Drill Instructor School at MCRD Parris Island (apparently the lessons didn't take).

Drilling Holes in the Sky
Flying; usually flying without a mission, often simply to obtain the necessary monthly flying time to be eligible for flight pay.

Drooping Turns
Helicopter pilot term for "I'm getting tired"; also when a helicopter is unable to maintain necessary rotor RPM for whatever reason.

Drownproofing
Survival swimming taught to every recruit.

Drum Major
Musician in charge of a band or musical unit; usually carries a baton used to signal changes in march and provide a tempo to the music; usually a staff noncommissioned officer.

Dry Fire
Simulated rifle fire used to teach correct positions for firing on the rifle range; also "Snap In."

DSS
Diplomatic Security Service; service within the State Department charged, among other things, with the security of embassies and consulates abroad; the "RSO" is a member of DSS.

Duck
See "Squid."

Dual Cool
Marine who is both parachute and scuba qualified, and wears the badges for both designations simultaneously; this term is usually used by someone who is, or wants to be, a jumper and diver.

Dual Fool
Marine who is both parachute and scuba qualified; the badges for both designations are usually worn simultaneously; this term is usually used by someone who thinks jumping out of airplanes and swimming beneath the sea is *crazy*.

Salty Language

Duty

> At work; on duty; having special requirements after normal working hours, i.e. units will have a Duty Officer, Duty NCO or Duty Driver; also the actual person, as in "Are you the Duty?"

DZ

> Drop Zone; designated landing area for parachutists.

Salty Language

Echo

Salty Language

EAS

End of Active Service; the date a Marine's enlistment is due to expire.

Eat Duck

Dine quickly; meaning "Duck in and duck out of the Mess Hall."

E-tool

Entrenching tool; small folding shovel with a multitude of field uses.

Eagle Globe and Anchor

Emblem of the United States Marine Corps; adopted in 1868 under Brigadier General Commandant Jacob Zeilen following the Civil War; prior to that time Marines had worn the Army infantry horn with a red field in the center and the letter "M" in Olde English script.

Eat the Apple, Fuck the Corps

Phrase used by Marines to express displeasure with the Marine Corps; usually mouthed by someone about to leave the Corps, or by a Marine who has endured a perceived injustice.

EGA

Abbreviation for Eagle Globe and Anchor; while it is certainly concise, it should *never* be used.

Elliott, George

Tenth Commandant of the Marine Corps; appointed Brigadier General Commandant to replace Major

General Commandant Heywood; served from Oct 3, 1903 to Nov 30, 1910; the law was changed on May 13, 1908 establishing the position of Major General Commandant - to which he was promoted.

Embassy Marine
Officially called a Marine Security Guard (MSG); Marine assigned to a State Department billet, usually at a United States embassy or consulate overseas.

Endex
The end of a field exercise; the end of *anything*.

Enlist
The act of joining the military services by individuals who are not becoming Warrant or Commissioned Officers.

Enlisted Marine
Marines in the rank of private, private first class and lance corporal; while all corporals and above are also enlisted, they are categorized as NCOs; also sometimes called a "Non-rate."

Epaulet
Shoulder decoration consisting of a strap which buttons near the collar.

EPW
Enemy Prisoner of War; also "POW."

Esprit de Corps
The "spirit" of a unit; commonly reflected by all of its history, traditions, and honor; pride.

EST

Essential Subjects Training; also "Essential Subjects Test."

Estrada, John L.

The Fifteenth Sergeant Major of the Marine Corps; serving from Jun 26, 2003.

Evening Parade

One hour and fifteen minute performance of music and precision marching; features "The President's Own" United States Marine Band, "The Commandant's Own," United States Marine Drum and Bugle Corps, and the Marine Corps Silent Drill Platoon; held every Friday evening from May through August; *not* to be confused with the "Sunset Parade."

EW

Electronic Warfare; the jamming of radio frequencies is a good example of EW.

Ewe

Female sheep; the only type of "You" a recruit should talk about while in boot camp; recruits always address their seniors in the third person, i.e. "This recruit requests permission to speak to the Drill Instructor"; this practice is also followed to some extent in the "Fleet," especially when addressing senior officers.

Ex-Marine

No such thing; once a Marine, always a Marine; see "Former Marine."

Exchange
See "Marine Corps Exchange."

Extended Port
Punitive position; recruits are ordered to "port arms" and then directed to extend their arms straight out in front until their elbows are not bent; in this position the weapon becomes heavy, and the arms ache.

Eye
What will get *put out* if a recruit refers to himself as "I" in the presence of his Drill Instructor; recruits refer to themselves in the third person, i.e. "The Recruit."

Eyeball
Look at.

Eyeball Liberty
Look at attractive women (or men, in the case of "WMs" and sailors)

Eye Corps
See "I Corps."

Eye Fuck
To look or stare at, usually in a curious manner.

Foxtrot

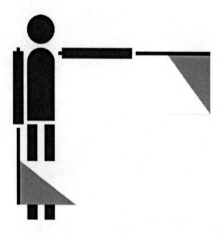

Salty Language

F-4 Phantom
Twin engine jet fighter/bomber used by Marines for ground support; replaced by the F/A-18 Hornet.

FAC
Forward Air Controller; someone who directs air strikes, either on the ground or aloft in an observation aircraft.

FAG
Field Artillery Group; now (thankfully) defunct; also a "Former Action Guy," i.e. a Marine whose job now requires him to man an "LMD" instead of deploying to the field.

Fail
Not used by Marines; this word has no place in the Corps; see "Quit."

Fantail
Open deck at the rear of a ship; usually where trash is dumped overboard.

FARP
Forward Arming and Refueling Point; gas station/ammo dump for aircraft out in the boonies.

Fartsack
Cover for a sleeping bag or mattress.

FAST
Fleet Anti-terrorism Support Team.

Fast Mover
Jet aircraft, especially fighter/bombers.

Fast Rope
(*n*) Special thick rope used to descend from a hovering helicopter; Marines wear heavy gloves and slide down as if it were a firehouse pole; (*v*) the act of descending to the ground using a fast rope.

Fat Body
Overweight person; also "Food Blister."

Fathom
Unit of depth measurement; essentially the distance between the fingers of outstretched arms; originally "faedm," an Anglo Saxon word meaning hug or embrace; fadems were marked on a rope with a knot so that when it was thrown overboard attached to an anchor, a sailor would count off the knots or fathoms to the bottom; one fathom equals six feet.

FDC
Fire Direction Center; the "brain" of an artillery unit.

Feather Merchant
Person of short stature or slight build; also person in a comfortable or easy assignment such as headquarters duty or some staff billet; often used for all civilians working for the military.

FEBA
Forward Edge of the Battle Area; the "front lines."

Feet Dry

Term used to indicate an aircraft has just crossed the beach and is now flying over dry land.

Feet Wet

Term used to indicate an aircraft has just crossed the beach and is now flying over the ocean.

FFAR

Folding-Fin Aerial Rockets; fired from aircraft; sometimes called "Free Flight Aerial Rocket" because they have no guidance system; usually refers to the 2.75-inch variety; see "Zuni."

FIDO

Fuck It, Drive On; keep going in spite of difficulty or discomfort; often used by Marines who have completed Army Ranger School.

Field Day

Day or evening set aside for the *very* thorough cleaning of barracks or offices; usually once a week while in garrison.

Field Expedient

Art of getting the job done despite limitations or lack of equipment; requires ingenuity; making something out of whatever is available

Field Grade

Commissioned officers in the grades of major, lieutenant colonel, and colonel.

Field Grade Good Conduct Medal
Derisive nickname for Bronze Star medal when it is awarded to Field Grade Officers without the "V" device; also "Officers' Good Conduct Medal."

Field Jacket
Cold weather coat; replaced by modern "Goretex" jacket.

Field Medical Service School (FMSS)
Often called "Devil Doc University"; it is where Navy corpsmen and dental technicians are trained for field duty with operational Marine Corps units.

Field Meet
Organized series of sporting competitions pitting one unit against another; organized grab ass.

Field Mess
See "Mess Night."

Field of Fire
Radius that an automatic weapon can cover in an arc from port to starboard.

Field Strip
Take apart or disassemble; as in field strip a rifle, or a cigarette butt.

Fieldscarf
Necktie worn with a Marine uniform.

Fighting Hole

Entrenched position for one or more Marines in a defensive situation; called a "Fox Hole" by the Army; Marines *never* use that term because you *hide* in a fox hole, and you *engage the enemy* from a fighting hole.

FIIGMO

Fuck It, I Got My Orders; often written "FIGMO"; used by someone who has received permanent change of station orders or is ending their term of service; either way they are "Short Timers," and don't much care about anything but leaving.

Final Strength Test

Physical fitness test given near the end of recruit training to determine if a recruit has improved sufficiently based upon the results of the "Initial Strength Test."

Fire For Effect

All guns in an artillery battery firing on a target at the same time; also means "Go ahead and do it."

Fire In The Hole

Alert that an explosive device is about to be detonated; if you hear this you probably missed all of the other warnings and are about to be blown away; also a warning that someone has just "broken wind."

Fire Team

Basic infantry fighting unit consisting of four Marines with various weapons and support; fire teams are combined into squads; in urban combat the fire team is frequently broken into two-man "buddy units."

Firebase
Forward artillery support position.

Fire Mission
The process of engaging a target with artillery.

Firewatch
A recruit's first introduction to guard duty; at least one recruit in each platoon remains awake and alert each night for safety and security purposes; when boot camp structures were made of wood, the posting was absolutely necessary, but since fireproof buildings were constructed starting in the 1960s the job has remained.

Firewatch Medal
National Defense Service Medal; awarded during time of war to every person in the military with 60 days of service; the theory behind the name is that in order to qualify for the NDSM all you have to do is stand one tour of duty as a "Firewatch."

First Lieutenant
Second grade of commissioned officer; indicated by a silver bar on the collar or epaulet of the uniform; pay grade is O-2.

First of foot and right of the line
Honor bestowed on the U. S. Marine Corps by the Secretary of the Navy on Aug. 9, 1876; it means Marines take the place of honor in any naval formation.

First Sergeant

Senior noncommissioned officer *billet* in a company or squadron; usually filled by a First Sergeant of Marines, but can be filled by whichever SNCO is senior in the event no Marine of that rank is assigned to a unit.

First Sergeant of Marines

Usually the senior noncommissioned officer in a company or squadron; indicated by three chevrons and three rockers with a diamond between chevrons and rockers, worn on each sleeve or collar point as appropriate; pay grade is E-8 (same as a master sergeant); the MOS of "9999" is sometimes jokingly called "unskilled labor" because gunnery sergeants promoted to first sergeant no longer work in their MOS and take on administrative duties which can theoretically be done by *any* competent SNCO.

First Shirt

First Sergeant.

First Skirt

Female First Sergeant.

First to Fight

Marines have been in the forefront of every American war since the founding of the Corps; they entered the Revolution in 1775, even before the Declaration of Independence was signed! Marines have carried out more than 300 landings on foreign shores, and have served everywhere from the Arctic to tropics; their record for readiness reflects pride, responsibility, and challenge; the Marine Corps is the only service which can be committed to battle on a large scale by the President without the express consent of Congress, which is a reflection of its expeditionary nature.

FitRep
Fitness Report; written on Marines in the rank of sergeant and above; measures his or her fitness for duty; it is the written report of a Marine's career, and is used to determine if a Marine should be promoted, retained or put into a position of increased responsibility.

Flag Allotment
Detachment of Marines assigned for security and various ceremonial purposes to certain Navy Admirals.

Flag Officer
Any of the general or admiral ranks, or any officer whose billet authorizes him to fly a personal flag (almost never applied in the present).

Flak Jacket
Forerunner of "Body Armor"; it would stop shrapnel, but not much else.

Flare Ship
C-47 twin-prop cargo plane which drops flares suspended from parachutes to provide nighttime illumination of a battle area; sometimes called "Spooky."

Fleet

A large group of ships, usually under the command of a flag officer; also "In the Fleet" is a term used to indicate the Marine Corps beyond boot camp and technical school; the "FMF."

Flight Line

Place on an airfield where aircraft are parked; also a mythical item which newbies to a unit are sent in quest of, i.e. "Go get me 100 feet of flight line."

Flight Surgeon

A physician and Navy Medical Officer who specializes in aviation medicine for both the Navy and Marine Corps.

Float

To be deployed at sea; usually with a MEU, as in a "six month float"; also the act of exchanging a broken piece of equipment for a new one.

Flotsam

Floating wreckage of a ship or its cargo; floating debris; unimportant miscellaneous material.

Fluff-n-buff

Cammies or utilities which were dried and not pressed (fluff dry), and boots which were brushed but not spit polished (buffed); the person wearing such an outfit is especially noticeable during inspections.

FM

Fucking magic: very high-tech; used to describe how something you don't understand actually works; often used in reference to "Frequency Modulated" radio gear.

FMJ
Full Metal Jacket; jacketed "ball" ammunition.

FMF
Fleet Marine Force; the REAL Marine Corps!

FNG
Fucking New Guy; a newbie.

FO
Forward Observer; usually an artillery officer assigned to infantry units to coordinate artillery support in support of Mud Marines.

FOD
Foreign Objects and Debris; a constant concern on airfields and carrier decks where jet engines operate; jet intakes can ingest loose objects, and even the smallest item – such as a rock or a bolt - can seriously damage turbine blades.

FOD Walk
Police call on a flight line; designed to rid it of "FOD."

Food Blister
Also "Fat Body"; someone who belongs in "PCP."

Fore
In front; from the naval term.

Forecastle
Open deck aboard most ships at the bow; usually where the anchors are secured; generally a place for off duty sailors to gather, tell sea stories and smoke (Pronounced *folk-sill*).

Formed
Reference to a unit of Marines under the control of someone while they are standing, walking, marching, sitting or even lying down in a prescribed manner; it is said that whenever two Marines are walking together, one is in command and the *other* is formed.

Forming Gang
A newly formed platoon of raw recruits.

Former Marine
Acceptable term for a Marine who is not currently serving; make no mistake, that person is *still* a Marine, and will *always* be a Marine.

Fortitudine
Original motto of the Marine Corps; Latin for "fortitude"; replaced by "Semper Fidelis."

Forty-five
See "45."

Forward Edge of the Battle Area (FEBA)
See "FEBA."

Four-deuce
4.2 inch mortar.

Four Holer
Field head consisting of four 55-gallon drums cut in half to expedite removal of fecal matter.

Foxhole
Army term for a "fighting hole."

Salty Language

FPF

Final Protective Fire; all weapons fired simultaneously at the cyclic rate to repel an enemy assault which has reached the "FPL."

FPL

Final Protective Line; point at which a position is about to be overrun; when the enemy reaches it, the "FPF" is fired.

Frag

(*n*) Fragmentation grenade; also (*v*) to kill a person of superior rank, usually by throwing a fragmentation grenade into the room or area where he or she is located (such as a hootch or a head); also a "fragmentary order," which gives subordinate commanders the information they require to conduct their portion of an operation.

Free Fire Zone

Area where anyone seen is assumed to be enemy and may be fired upon.

French Fourragere

Rope worn around the left shoulder by the 5th and 6th Marine Regiments; the government of France honored those units, along with the now-defunct 6th Machinegun Battalion, with the Fourragere for their valor during World War I; those units still wear the award today; called a "Pogey Rope" by those who don't rate it.

Salty Language

Frock
> Assume next higher grade without a pay raise; used when a Marine needs to be a certain rank in order to fill a billet; only done when the Marine in question has already been selected by HQMC for promotion to that grade, and is waiting for his seniority number to come up.

Frog
> Nickname for the CH-46 helicopter; given because the rear portion of the aircraft sits lower than the front like a squatting frog; some spell it "Phrog"; also a device used to suspend a sword from a belt.

Front Leaning Rest Position
> The position for pushups; often simply, "the position."

Frozen Chosin
> See "Chosin Reservoir."

FSMAO
> Field Supply Maintenance Analysis Office; the name of an inspection which occurs to all units periodically; it is the cause of a lot of "Pencil Whipping"; now called "The Marine Corps Logistics Chain Analysis Team" (a good example of "Rock Painting"); many salty Marines still call it "FSMAO" (Pronounced *phase-mow*).

FSSG
> Force Service Support Group; the part of a MEF which supplies and maintains a Marine division; sometimes called "Fumble, Stumble, Stagger and Glide" by line units.

FTA
Fuck the Army.

FTN
Fuck the Navy.

FTS
Full Time Support; a reservist who is on active duty as part of an "I&I Staff."

FUBAB
Fucked (or "Fouled") Up Beyond All Belief.

FUBAR
Fucked (or "Fouled") Up Beyond All Recognition; another version is "Fucked Up Beyond All Repair."

Fuck You Bird
Bird indigenous to Southeast Asia whose call sounds exactly like, "fuck you."

Fuller, Ben H.
Fifteenth Commandant of the Marine Corps; appointed Major General Commandant upon the death of Wendell Neville, July 9, 1930; served until Feb. 28, 1934.

Funeral Pace
Pace of march for funerals; approximately half the pace of quick time.

Golf

Salty Language

G-1
Division or Wing Personnel Office or Officer.

G-2
Division or Wing Intelligence Office or Officer; also a common reference to a person's intelligence.

G-3
Division or Wing Operations and Training Office/Officer.

G-4
Division or Wing Logistics Office or Officer.

G-Spot
Building containing the majority of the division staff organizations (designated G-1, G-2, G-3 etc.) at Camp Pendleton, CA.

GAF
Give A Fuck.

Gaff Off
Ignore.

Gaggle
A disorganized group.

Gaggle Fuck
See "Cluster Fuck."

Gale, Anthony
Fourth Commandant of the Marine Corps; Gale's short tenure as Lieutenant Colonel Commandant was punctuated by the dislike of the Secretary of the Navy, who charged him in a court martial; the specifications included, "being intoxicated in common dram shops and other places of low repute"; found guilty and sentenced to dismissal from the service; his place of burial is unknown; the only Commandant for whom no likeness exists.

Galley
Kitchen.

Gamma Goat
Unusual truck and trailer combination; very difficult to drive; supposedly amphibious; no longer used by the Marine Corps.

Gangway
(v) Order to clear space to make way for an approaching senior officer or official party; see "Make A Hole"; *(n)* a ladder or ramp used to board and debark a ship.

Garbage Burner
Unofficial name given to the M67A2 Flame Thrower Tank, since it was used mostly to burn garbage dumps in Vietnam.

Garrison
Any place civilized comforts, such as showers and cots, can be found; not in the boonies.

Salty Language

Garrison Cover
Uniform cover invented in the 20th Century; consists of a cap running fore and aft on the head; displays the eagle globe and anchor on the front left, and the rank insignia of commissioned and warrant officers on the right; no rank is worn by enlisted personnel; also called "Pisscutter" or "Cunt Cap."

Gas Chamber
Building used for training Marines in the actions to be taken during a Nuclear, Biological or Chemical attack; various gases are used in training (usually CS); all of them are noxious - but none are fatal.

Gator
Amphibious ship used to transport and land Marines, i.e. LHA, LPH, LST, LSD, LPD; the all-inclusive name is "Gator Navy."

Gear
Things; personal things such as clothing and equipment, or unit things such as 782 gear; essentially, *all* things.

Gear Adrift
Anything not properly stowed, tied down or otherwise secured.

Geedunk
Snack bar on ship; any place candy and "Pogey Bait" are sold; also the candy itself.

Geeters
Money.

General
Highest rank in the Marine Corps; the Commandant of the Marine Corps is a general; pay grade is O-10; designated by four silver stars worn on collar points or epaulets.

General Officers
Commissioned Officers in the ranks of brigadier general, major general, lieutenant general and general; also called "Flag Officers" because federal law authorizes a flag to be flown whenever a general officer is present or aboard.

General Orders
There are eleven general orders for guard duty; *every* Marine must memorize them:

1. To take charge of this post and all government property in view.
2. To walk my post in a military manner, keeping always on the alert and observing everything that takes place within sight or hearing.
3. To report all violations of orders I am instructed to enforce.
4. To repeat all calls from posts more distant from the guardhouse than my own.
5. To quit my post only when properly relieved.
6. To receive, obey, and pass on to the sentry who relieves me, all orders from the commanding officer, officer of the day, and officers and noncommissioned officers of the guard only.
7. To talk to no one except in the line of duty.
8. To give the alarm in case of fire or disorder.
9. To call the corporal of the guard in any case not

covered by instructions.
10. To salute all officers and all colors and standards not cased.
11. To be especially watchful at night and during the time for challenging, to challenge all persons on or near my post, and to allow no one to pass without proper authority.

General Quarters

Highest condition of alert aboard ship; pulls the crew from normal work assignments to a warfighting stance; in the days of wooden ships with rigging, a portion of the Marine Detachment would report to the rigging as sharpshooters, while others would report to a gun crew; in the modern Navy, Marines would usually man one or more guns (which were usually painted with an eagle globe and anchor, and were generally know to have the highest accuracy of all gun crews); since 1998 there have been no Marines assigned as a permanent part of any ship's crew.

Get a Hat

Leave.

Get Some

Kill the enemy; have sex; engage in *any* activity with enthusiasm.

Ghost Turds

Dust balls; Blanket lint, much like drier lint, which accumulates on the deck as if by magic.

GI Bill
Originally the "GI Bill of Rights"; financial assistance provided to people who have served, or are serving, in the military; for educational and home purchasing purposes; Administered by the Department of Veterans Affairs.

GI Can
Galvanized Iron Can; garbage can; also "Shitcan."

Gig
Discrepancy.

Gigahertz and Nanoseconds
Highly technical, detailed, and hard to understand; i.e. "It's getting down to gigahertz and nanoseconds."

Gig Line
The military alignment of the shirt flap, belt buckle, and trouser fly; if they are not aligned, it is considered a "Gig."

GI Shower
Given to someone who usually is in need of a shower, but refuses to take one; the offender is forced into the shower, where others scrub him with scrub brushes and/or steel wool; the intent is to encourage the individual to maintain minimal standards of cleanliness; the outcome is often painful, and even bloody; an illegal assault punishable under the UCMJ; rarely happens.

Gitmo
Guantanamo Bay, Cuba.

GMT

Greenwich Mean Time; see "Zulu Time."

Go Ashore

Leave the ship; leave the base; go home; go on liberty.

Go Juice

Fuel, gasoline, diesel, JP, etc.; also "coffee."

Goat Heads

Thorns indigenous to California; on field exercises they stick to everything, and are a major nuisance.

Goat Locker

Navy Chief Petty Officer's quarters; from the naval tradition in which goats brought aboard for milk were under the charge of the chiefs.

Goat Rope

Similar to a "Cluster Fuck," except that this activity comes directly from the "Head Shed."

Gobbler

Female in a "Turkey Bar" who provides oral sex for a fee.

God Box

Chapel.

Gofasters

Running shoes; sneakers.

Gold Wing Ceremony

Rite of passage during which a new "Gold Winger" is awarded his "Blood Wings"; the clutch backs are removed from a pair of wings, and they are pounded into the Marine's chest by a minimum of ten "Gold Wingers."

Gold Wings

Navy/Marine Corps Parachutist Insignia; far more prestigious than the "Lead Sled"; awarded to Marines filling paid jump billets who have met certain qualifications; differ from "Wings of Gold," which designate Naval aviators; see "Blood Wings" and "Lead Sled."

Gold Winger

Marine who rates gold parachute wings.

Good Conduct Medal (GCM)

Individual award given to an enlisted Marine for three consecutive years of undetected crime while on active duty.

Good Cookie

Marine Corps "Good Conduct Medal."

Good to Go

Means "I am ready" or "the piece of equipment is ready" or that despite what may appear to be obstacles, "the mission will be completed"; also indicates approval of something or someone, as in "You are good to go."

Gook
Pejorative term for anyone of Asian extraction, particularly an enemy (i.e. North Korean, North Vietnamese, etc).

GORETEX
Fabric specifically engineered to form an impenetrable barrier against wind and water while maintaining breathability; what Marines call their cold/wet weather gear.

Gorilla Cookie
Big chocolate cookie contained in some "MREs."

Gouge, The
A takeoff on "scoop"; it suggest that *this* information is from a *reliable* source.

Gourd
Human head; also "Melon" and Grape."

GP Tent
General Purpose Tent; large canvas tent; usually used to billet troops in a rear area while in the field.

Grabass
Horsing around.

Grade
Relative position of a person to other persons of similar rank; see "pay grade."

Grape
A person's head; also "Gourd" and "Melon."

Gray, Alfred M. Jr.
Twenty-ninth Commandant of the Marine Corps; served from July 1, 1987 until June 30, 1991; a "Mustang" known for being plain spoken, he wore cammies in his official photo instead of Alphas and drank coffee from a camouflage canteen cup to which four stars had been affixed; affectionately called "Big Al" by the troops (but *never* to his face).

Grease
Kill.

Grease Gun
See "M3A1."

Green Eye
Starlight Scope; first generation of night vision equipment; first used in Vietnam, it was very large and very heavy.

Green Machine
Derogatory term used by Marines referring to the Marine Corps; also used regularly by soldiers to proudly describe the Army.

Green Side Out
See "Brown Side Out."

Green Weenie
Sometimes "Big Green Weenie"; it's what the Marine Corps uses to screw you.

Greene, Wallace M.
Twenty-third Commandant of the Marine Corps; served from Jan. 1, 1964 until Dec. 31, 1967.

Greenwich Mean Time (GMT)
See "Zulu Time."

Grid Square
A standard grid square on a military map; 1000 meters by 1000 meters; they do *not* come in boxes!

Grinder
A large field, usually paved, upon which formations and parades are held; see "Parade Deck."

Grog
Alcoholic beverage issued to sailors and Marines aboard ships until the Civil War; the recipe varied, but was most commonly half rum and half water; the inspiration for "1775 Rum Punch"; see "Splice the Main Brace."

Ground Guide
Someone who walks in front of a tank or AAV in congested areas and guides it using hand signals.

Ground Pounder
Infantryman; grunt.

Group
Sub-division of an Air Wing; equivalent to a regiment in infantry terms.

Group Tighteners
Non-existent "search & fetch" item for rookies, a-la "Bucket of Steam"; also a placebo drop of solvent or oil placed upon the weapon sights of an unsuspecting marksmanship trainee by a range instructor as a last

127

resort to instill confidence and get the idiot qualified; also adult beverages employed by competitive marksmen to either relax after a day of dealing with recruits, or combat match butterflies prior to competing.

Grunt
Infantryman; originally a pejorative term, but now a source of pride.

GU11
Navy version of the Air Force "B1RD."

Guide
Person responsible for the unit "Guidon"; the individual upon whom a unit "forms up" for a formation.

Guidon
Official pennant of a platoon or company; at the battalion or squadron level or above, units have official "Colors."

Gun
Artillery or other weaponry in which the barrel does not contain rifling (lands and grooves); also used for machineguns, i.e. "Guns up!"; *never* used in reference to a rifle or pistol!

Gun Bunny
Pejorative term for someone in the field artillery; also a "Cannon Cocker."

Gun Deck
Falsify documents, reports, or records.

Salty Language

Gung Ho

Eager and ready to accomplish whatever task necessary; the term was originally brought back from China by Colonel Evans Carlson; literally translated from the Chinese, it means "working in harmony" or "working together"; it became the motto of the "Marine Raiders."

Gungy

Gung Ho, but usually in an inexperienced, just-out-of-recruit-training way.

Gunner

Marine warrant officer in the MOS 0306 Infantry Weapons Officer; name often given to all warrant officers, but that is incorrect; a *true* Gunner will replace the insignia of rank on his right collar with a bursting bomb insignia; see also "Lipstick Lieutenant"; name also applies to an enlisted machine gunner (MOS 0331).

Gunnery Sergeant of Marines

Noncommissioned officer in pay grade E-7; wears three chevrons and two rockers with crossed rifles between them on both sleeves or collar points as appropriate; often called "Gunny" by the troops, or "Guns" by contemporaries and seniors.

Gunny

Informal term for a gunnery sergeant; also what members of the State Department call *all* MSG "DetCmdrs."

Guns
Gunnery sergeant; not generally used by junior Marines.

GWOT
Global War on Terrorism.

Gyrene
Diminutive form of "Marine"; seldom used by Marines.

Hotel

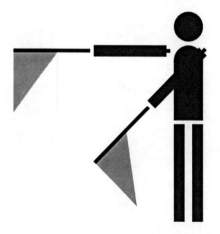

Salty Language

H-34

UH-34 resupply and medevac helicopter; used in Vietnam.

H&I

Harassment and Interdiction artillery fire; designed to limit and/or alter enemy movement.

H&S

Headquarters and Service Company, (or Battalion); sometimes called "Hide and Slide" or "Huck and Suck."

Hack It, or Pack It

Cut the mustard, or pack your trash!

Hagee, Michael W.

Thirty-Third Commandant of the Marine Corps; serving from Jan 14, 2003 to the present.

Haj

Iraqi citizen;. a local (usually a good guy); also "Haggie" (from the Johnny Quest cartoon); supposedly means friend; also **"Haji"** or "Haci."

Half Step

Fifteen-inch step in marching; also to take half measures; not applying yourself fully.

HALO

High Altitude Low Opening; see "MFF."

Halazone
Water purification tablet.

HAM
Hairy Assed Marine; female response to "BAM."

Ham and Motherfuckers
Ham and Lima Beans; the most reviled C-ration meal; so bad you usually couldn't even give it away to the locals; the meal included apricots; sometimes called the "dead man's meal" because it was said that if you ate apricots before going into battle you would be hit.

Hamlet
Village of less than 100 residents.

HANO
High Altitude *No* Opening; what happens when a "HALO" jump goes bad; see "MFF."

Happy Birthday
Greeting exchanged by Marines on 10 November; also a greeting to a Marine by a non-Marine on that date.

Hard Charger
Motivated Marine.

Harper's Ferry
Location of John Brown's ill-fated uprising in 1859, and of his capture by U. S. Marines under the command of Army Lieutenant Colonel Robert E.

Lee; the Marines were led by Lieutenant Israel Greene, who would later resign his commission to join the Confederate States Marines; Marine Private Luke Quinn was killed when he breached a hole in the firehouse door and was shot by John Brown; he can arguably be considered the first casualty of the Civil War.

Harrier
AV-8B VTOL (Vertical Takeoff and Landing) jet aircraft; it is unique to the Marine Corps in the U.S. Armed Forces.

Harris, John
Sixth Commandant of the Marine Corps; became Colonel Commandant on the death of long-serving Archibald Henderson; served through the Civil War; died in office on May 12, 1864.

Hashmark
Service Stripes worn on forearm of dress and service uniforms by enlisted Marines; each denotes 4 years of service.

Hashmark Private
Private with more than four years of service; they have no chevrons denoting rank, but *do* rate one or more service stripes; common in the "Old Corps," when promotions were much slower than they are today; in modern times most certainly a Marine who has been "Busted" all the way down to "Slick Sleeve."

HASP
Hawaiian Armed Services Police.

Hat
Informal term for the Campaign Cover worn by Drill Instructors; also an informal name for the Drill Instructors themselves.

Hatch
Door.

Havelock
Civilian community outside the main gate of MCAS Cherry Point, NC; also a cloth hanging from the back of a cap or hat to protect the neck (a la the French Foreign Legion).

HE
High Explosive.

Head
Latrine or toilet; from the naval term; in the sailing navy the forecastle (pronounced *folk-sill*) was the forward most deck open to the weather; one corner of the forecastle, with a wide scupper, was where sailors went to the bathroom; as the forecastle was in the front or "head" of the ship, a sailor on the way to relieve himself would declare that he was "on the way to the head."

Head Shed
Headquarters or Command Post where all of the leaders are gathered; the wheelhouse; puzzle palace; a great place for enlisted Marines to stay *away* from.

Heart
    Short for the "Purple Heart Medal;" given for wounds received in action; the one medal you *don't* want!

Heat Tab
    Fuel for a C-Ration Stove; a tablet of blue Trioxin, which causes fumes which irritate the eyes and respiratory tract if ventilation holes aren't large enough; with a properly vented stove only half a Trioxin heat tab was needed to heat the meal, and then the other half could be used to heat water for coffee or cocoa; a small chunk of C-4 explosive could also be substituted for the Trioxin tablet for faster heating; also a nickname for the "Sun."

Heavy
    The Junior Drill Instructor assigned to a recruit platoon; responsible for teaching COD and strict(er) enforcement of discipline; also called the "Heavy Hat."

Helo
    Helicopter.

Hide and Slide
    See "H&S."

HLZ
    Helicopter Landing Zone; also called an "LZ."

Henderson, Archibald

Fifth Commandant of the Marine Corps; known as the "Grand Old Man of the Corps," as he served longest in the position - 38 years; served as Acting Commandant from Sept. 16, 1818 until Gale's appointment on March 3, 1819; named Lieutenant Colonel Commandant at the conclusion of Gale's court martial which cashiered him from the service on Oct. 17, 1820; during Henderson's tenure he led Marines in the Indian Wars in Florida, reportedly tacking a note to the door of the Commandant's House saying, "Gone to fight the Indians, be back when the war is over"; also became the first Colonel Commandant; awarded a Brevet promotion to Brigadier General.

Henderson Hall

Building in Arlington VA close to the Pentagon; used to house enlisted Marines assigned to HQMC at the Pentagon and other administrative functions; named for Brevet Brigadier General, Colonel Commandant Archibald Henderson, the "Grand Old Man of the Corps."

HEPT

High Explosive Plastic Tracer; type of tank round.

Herk

C-130 Hercules transport aircraft.

Herringbone

World War II fabric in a field green color; used to make utility uniforms; phased out during Korea; by the time of Vietnam they were worn only by real "Salts."

Heywood, Charles
Ninth Commandant of the Marine Corps; became Colonel Commandant on Jan. 30, 1891 and served in the position until Oct. 2, 1903.

Hide and Slide
See "H&S"; also to "Skate."

High and Tight
Traditional Marine haircut; it is basically a flattop with whitewalls.

High and To the Right
Really, *really* pissed off; as in, "The Gunny went high and to the right when he found out you were UA!"; the term comes from where rounds impact on a target when the shooter jerks the trigger.

Hip Pocket Promotion
Promotion given to a Marine "on the spot" by a General Officer; so called because the general seemingly pulls the promotion warrant out of his hip pocket; also called a "Spot" or "Pocket" promotion; they are rare.

Hiyoko
To "bug out" in a big hurry.

HMFIC
Head Mother Fucker In Charge; see "MFICC."

HMMWV
High Mobility Multi-Wheeled Vehicle (pronounced *hum-vee*); also called a "Hummer."

HMX-1
Marine Executive Helicopter Squadron One; based at Quantico VA; the squadron which flies and maintains the Presidential helicopter(s), i.e. "Marine One."

Hog Board
See "Pig Board."

Holcomb, Thomas
Seventeenth Commandant of the Marine Corps; named Major General Commandant on Dec. 1, 1936; on Jan. 20, 1942 a new law required the Commandant to be a Lieutenant General, and provided that the title be "Commandant of the Marine Corps," dropping the reference to rank; retired from the Marine Corps on Dec. 31, 1943 and the next day was promoted to General on the retired list (See "Tombstone Brigadier General"); the first Marine to hold that rank.

Hole
Window; from the naval term "Porthole"; see "Make a Hole."

Hollywood Marine
Marines trained at MCRD San Diego, CA; it is rumored among Parris Island Marines that Hollywood Marines are issued sunglasses in boot camp; there are no female Hollywood Marines; all females go through boot camp in the 4th Recruit Training Battalion (formerly WM Battalion) at MCRD Parris Island, S.C.

Honcho
Person in charge who is not necessarily *assigned* to be in charge; see "HMFIC."

Honey Bucket
Any bucket used to clean out a toilet; usually carried in pairs on a stick by Asian women and men.

Hooch
Hard liquor; usually contraband; often homemade.

Hook Up
Get in touch with.

Hootch
Living quarters; originally occupied by enlisted Marines; the word later become a general term for *wherever* a Marine is living.

Hornet
The F/A-18 "Hornet" is a single- and two-seat, twin engine, multi-mission fighter/attack aircraft which can operate from either aircraft carriers or land bases; fills a variety of roles: air superiority, fighter escort, suppression of enemy air defenses, reconnaissance, forward air control, close and deep air support, and day and night strike missions; replaced the F-4 Phantom, A-7 Corsair II and A-6 Intruder.

Horse Blanket
Thick wool blanket; also a nickname for the heavy green wool overcoat once issued to all Marines and seldom worn.

Horse Cock
Lunch meat; becomes a "Horsecock Sandwich" when placed between two slices of bread; often the main component of a "Bag Nasty."

Horse Marines
See "China Marines."

Hospital Corners
Method of making a rack where the top blanket is squared off, leaving one 45 degree angle on each corner; this allows the blanket to be tucked under, making it straight and tight.

Hostess House
On-base hotel for guests of Marines.

Hotel Street
Vice district of Honolulu, Hawaii during WWII; contained 20 brothels and around 200 prostitutes.

House Mouse
Recruit who provides assistance to the drill instructor in the form of keeping the drill instructor hut tidy, along with other minor tasks and chores.

Housewife
Sewing kit (archaic).

HQ
Headquarters.

HQMC
Headquarters Marine Corps; located in the Pentagon; previously at the Navy Annex, on a plot of land where the Air Force Monument will be built (The original site for the AF Monument was on Arlington Ridge adjacent to the Marine Corps War Memorial, but Marines and their friends fought *that* placement as inappropriate).

Huck and Suck
See "H&S."

Huey
UH-1 Iroquois helicopter; utility helo used extensively by the Marine Corps, especially in Vietnam.

Hummer
See "HMMWV."

Hump
Field march or extended hike; to carry something.

Hurt Locker
A bad situation; i.e. "I'm in a real hurt locker."

Huss
Give me a break or help me out; i.e. "Cut me a huss."

India

I

What a recruit is *not*; see "Eye."

I.M.R.

Individual Memorandum of Receipt; form used to issue "782 Gear."

I&I

Inspector and Instructor; active duty cadre assigned to a Marine Corps reserve unit.

I Corps

Most northern of four Corps areas into which South Vietnam was divided; it was adjacent to the DMZ; I Corps was Marine territory, while the Army controlled II, III and IV Corps (Pronounced *eye-core*).

IBGB

Itty Bitty Gook Boats; small Vietnamese fishing junks in the DaNang area; early in the 1960s they were prevalent, but by the end of the decade they were nearly extinct.

IED

Improvised Explosive Device; modern version of a "Booby Trap"; usually command detonated.

IFR

Instrument Flight Rules; permits safe flight in conditions of limited visibility when "VFR" is not possible; also the simplistic method of navigation used by some pilots, i.e. "I Follow the Roads."

IG
Inspector General.

Ike Jacket
Term which was not authorized in the Marine Corps; when used, it would subject a Marine to reprimand; Marines remembered General Eisenhower's comment that he would have no Marines in Europe (having forgotten that his reserve force in Northern Ireland was Marine, and paying no attention to the OSS personnel in-theater); a uniform jacket of similar design was authorized just after WWII and continued into the early 1960s; see "Battle Jacket."

Illum
Illumination; night artillery fire used to illuminate an area using a phosphorous filament suspended by a parachute.

Improvise, Adapt and Overcome
Unofficial mantra of the Marine Corps; based on the fact the Corps often received Army hand-me-downs, and the troops were poorly equipped; despite this, the Marine Corps has been successful largely because of this attitude; the phrase was popularized by "Gunny Highway" in the Clint Eastwood movie "Heartbreak Ridge."

In-Country
Serving in a combat zone, especially in Vietnam or Iraq.

In the Fleet
See "Fleet."

Incentive Training
Physical exercise used as a punishment to instill motivation, particularly in a Marine recruit during boot camp; also called "quarterdecking," or "being pitted" (outside it is usually conducted in a special sand pit designed for that purpose); also called "Incentive PT."

Incendiary
Artillery shell which burns upon impact; usually filled with white phosphorous.

Incoming
Alert that something is coming at or toward you, often enemy fire or artillery.

Indian Territory
Enemy held areas.

Infantry Training Battalion (ITB)
See "School of Infantry."

Initial Strength Test
Physical test given early in the training of a recruit to determine if he or she meets minimum fitness standards; a baseline for measuring progress.

Ink Stick
Pen (writing instrument).

Irish Pennant

String hanging randomly from a Marine's uniform; longer ones are sometimes called rappelling ropes or cables; a "Squared Away" Marine will be free of Irish pennants, particularly at an inspection; originated after World War II, and refers to the green-colored service or class A uniform due to the connection between the Irish and the color green; also called a "Russian Rope."

Iron Mike

Statue of a World War I Marine at Quantico, VA, with a copy at Parris Island; the original was made by the government of France to thank Americans for their aid in World War I. When it was presented to General Pershing he noticed the Doughboy holding aloft an M1911 pistol had a Marine Corps emblem on his helmet. Pershing refused to accept the sculpture, and it was given to the Marines.

IT

Incentive Training.

ITB

Infantry Training Battalion; see "School of Infantry."

ITR

Infantry Training Regiment; the old name for "Infantry Training Battalion."

Iwakuni

MCAS at Iwakuni, Japan; home of the 1st Marine Air Wing; also known as "Kuni."

Juliet

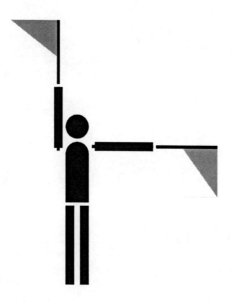

Salty Language

Jacksonville
Civilian community adjacent to Camp Lejeune, NC; commonly called "J'ville."

JAG
Judge Advocate General; head of the legal branch of the military services; military lawyers are generally called "JAGs" in reference to their serving in the JAG's organization; also, a *ridiculous* TV show about military lawyers (including one female Marine officer).

Jammer
See "Career Planner."

Jarhead
A pejorative term for a Marine; one account suggests it refers to the Marine "high and tight" haircut; another legend says that during World War II the Mason Jar Company stopped making jars in order to make helmets for Marines; also the title of an *awful* book and movie about Marines during the Gulf War.

Jerry Can
Five-gallon metal can designed for transporting gasoline and other volatile liquids; see "Donkey Dick."

Jetsam
The part of a ship, its equipment, or cargo which is cast overboard to lighten the load in time of distress.

Jibs
Teeth; as in, "I'll bust you in the jibs."

JOB
See "Junk on the Bunk" inspection; also called "Things on the Springs."

Jody
Traditionally, the civilian who moves in on your girl while you are serving in the Marine Corps.

Joe
Coffee; *origin*: Josephus Daniels was appointed Secretary of the Navy by President Woodrow Wilson in 1913. Among his reforms was the abolishment of the officers' wine mess. From that time on the strongest drink aboard Navy ships was coffee, and over the years a cup of coffee became known as "a cup of Joe."

Joe Shit the Rag Man
The generic screw up; an un-squared away Marine; also an unknown or undesignated person; everyman.

John Wayne
Tool included in each case of C-Rations; used to open the cans; see "P-38."

Joint Chiefs of Staff (JCS)
Department of Defense organization consisting of the Chiefs of Staff of the Army and Air Force, the Chief of Naval Operations, and the Commandant of the Marine Corps.

Jones, James L.
Thirty-second Commandant of the Marine Corps; served July 1, 1999 to Jan 13, 2003.

Jungle Boots
Boots designed for a jungle environment; made from standard field boots, with the upper leather replaced by a breathable canvas which will dry while being worn; the sole was reinforced with a steel shank in response to the threat of Punji Sticks.

Jungle Bunny
Grunt; infantryman; used in Vietnam.

Junior Drill Instructor
See "Drill Instructor."

Junk on the bunk
Inspection of a Marine's uniforms and equipment where everything is laid out in a specified order on the bunk; also called a "J.O.B." or "Things on the Springs."

J'ville
See "Jacksonville N.C."

Salty Language

Kilo

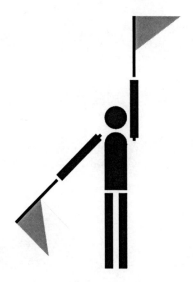

Salty Language

K-Bar
Standard Marine Corps fighting knife.

K-Bay
MCAS (Helicopter) Kaneohe Bay, Oahu, Hawaii; now called "MCBH."

K-rations
Individual field rations during World War II; universally detested for their lack of taste and rubbery consistency; replaced by "C-rations."

Kaibosh
Cancel; cause something to stop; i.e. "Put the kaibosh on."

KIA
Killed in Action.

Kelley, Paul X.
Twenty-eighth Commandant of the Marine Corps; served from July 1, 1983 until June 30, 1987.

Kin Ville
Small town outside of Camp Hansen in the northern part of Okinawa; sometimes called "Sin-ville" because of the large number of bars and imported bar girls there.

King Neptune
Mythological God of the Sea; he always presides, with his court, at "Line-Crossing Ceremonies."

Kiwi®
The preferred brand of shoe polish for Marines since World War II; also the national bird of New Zealand, and a nickname for a New Zealander.

Kiwi Assist
A good, sharp, kick in the ass.

Knot
Speed through the air or water; nautical miles per hour.

Klick
See "Click."

KP
Kitchen Police; term used mostly by the Army; duty assigned to junior enlisted Marines, sometimes as punishment; usually called "Mess Duty."

Krulak, Charles C.
Thirty-first Commandant of the Marine Corps; served from July 1, 1995 until June 30, 1999; son of Lieutenant General Victor "Brute" Krulak.

Kuni
MCAS Iwakuni, Japan.

Lima

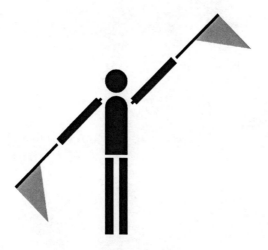

Salty Language

Salty Language

Ladder
Stairs; also "Ladderway" or "Ladderwell."

Laminated Light Duty Chit
Something which *seems* to be possessed by Marines with long-term injuries, or a series of injuries or illnesses; see "Light Duty Chit."

Lance Coolie
Lance Corporal.

Lance Corporal
Rank between private first class and corporal; not a noncommissioned officer rank; the insignia is a single chevron with crossed rifles beneath it worn on each sleeve or collar point of the uniform; pay grade is E-3; often nicknamed a "Lance Coolie" because they do most of the manual labor along with PFCs and privates.

Landing Party Manual (LPM)
The complete book of what to do and when to do it which guided the Marine Corps through most of the 20th Century; although now obsolete, copies are prized by professional Marines for the wealth of information and simple approach to leadership, morale, discipline, warfighting and professionalism.

Lash Up
Unit or organization; no longer used.

LAAW
Light Antitank Assault Weapon; rocket with a shaped-charge warhead contained in a collapsible, disposable fiberglass tube; sometimes spelled "LAW."

LAV
Light Armored Vehicle; 8x8 wheeled all-terrain, all-weather vehicle; comes in light armored combat, combat support, and combat service support versions; air transportable, and fully amphibious; the combat variant is armed with a 25-mm chain gun.

Lay Chilly
Freeze; stop all motion.

LBE
Load Bearing Equipment; usually "web gear" worn by infantry personnel to hold packs and tools and weapons and first aid kits and whatever *else* is worn by a Marine in the field.

LBFM
Little Brown Fucking Machine; pejorative term for the South Pacific island girls Marines encounter on liberty.

LBV
Load Bearing Vest; vest which holds magazines of ammunition, grenades and a cartridge belt, to which is attached other equipment such as first aid kit and canteens; see "782 Gear."

LCAC
Landing Craft Air Cushion; large landing craft capable of carrying tanks; skims over the water.

LCM
Landing Craft Mechanized; large landing craft used to transport armored vehicles to the beach.

LCVP
> Landing Craft Vehicle and Personnel; small landing craft used to transport Marines from ship to shore.

LDO
> Limited Duty Officer; CWOs and senior enlisted people who are commissioned as officers in order to serve as technical managers in their MOS.

Lead Sled
> Basic Parachutist Wings; pewter in color, with the corners of the wings curled up; worn by the Army, and Marines who have graduated from Airborne training but have not qualified for "Gold Wings."

Lead Turd
> Bad idea; an idea that is going nowhere *fast*.

LEAPEX
> A jump-through-your-ass project, exercise, or drill; a short-fused tasking which needs to be done *now!*

Leatherneck
> A Marine; comes from the early days of the Marine Corps when enlisted men were given strips of leather to wear around their necks; some say the leather was to protect the neck from a saber slash, while others believe it was to keep the Marines from slouching in uniform by forcing them to keep their head up; whichever it is, it makes for a great nickname!

Leatherneck Magazine
> Magazine published for Marines by the Marine Corps Association.

Leatherneck Square
  Area south of the DMZ in Vietnam with the following outposts as its corners: Con Tien (NW), Cam Lo Hill (SW), Cua Viet (SE) and Gia Linh (NE).

Leave
  Authorized absence from duty; different from liberty; Marines earn 30 days of leave each year.

Lee, Lewis G.
  Thirteenth Sergeant Major of the Marine Corps; served from June 30, 1995 until June 30, 1999.

Leftwich Trophy
  Trophy for Outstanding Leadership presented annually to a Marine Corps captain serving with the ground forces of the Fleet Marine Force; named in honor of Lieutenant Colonel William Groom Leftwich, Jr., who was KIA attempting to extract one of his beleaguered Recon teams in Vietnam.

Leggings
  Canvas, leather or cloth bindings; strapped, buckled, tied or wrapped to the ankles for support; used to keep out mud, snow and water; by the Korean War the Army had abandoned use of them, but the Marine Corps retained them for their distinctive look. When a dispatch from a Chinese general was found in which he had ordered his troops not to engage the "yellow legs," but to instead seek out the less fierce Army units, Marines were ordered to stop wearing their leggings.

Lejeune, John Archer
Thirteenth Commandant of the Marine Corps; legendary World War I commander; first Marine to command an Army division; first appointed Major General Commandant on July 1, 1920; first Commandant to be reappointed, serving until March 4, 1929; His birthday message to the Corps must be read each 10 November, by order.

LES
Leave and Earnings Statement; military version of a "pay stub."

Letter of Appreciation
Lowest form of official commendation; it can come from virtually *anyone*.

Letter of Commendation
Commendation which is higher a "Meritorious Mast," but below the level of a personal decoration; usually signed by a Commanding General.

Letterhead BG
See "Tombstone Brigadier General."

LHA
Landing Helicopter Assault ship; sometimes jokingly referred to as a "Luxury Hotel Afloat."

Liberty
Authorized absence from duty; usually the time when not at work or on duty; granted by the local commander, and may be as long as 96 consecutive hours; does not count as leave.

Liberty Call
The time when liberty commences.

Liberty Hound
Marine who is thought to be over-consumed with liberty; see "1631."

LIC
Low Intensity Conflict; the "Banana Wars" were a good example of a LIC.

Lick 'em and Stick 'em
Placing paper patches over holes in targets in the butts; the papers were once coated with water-activated glue, which had to be licked before sticking on the target.

Lid
Acceptable word for a "Cover."

Lieutenant Colonel
Fifth grade of commissioned officer; indicated by a silver oak leaf on the collar or epaulet of the uniform; pay grade is O-5; sometimes informally called a "Light Colonel."

Lieutenant General
Third flag officer rank; indicated by three silver stars on the collar or epaulet of the uniform; pay grade is O-9.

Lifer
A person intending to serve on active duty until retirement; one with extensive experience; some snuffies believe it stands for "Lazy Inefficient Fuckoff Expecting Retirement"; see "Refil."

Lifer Juice
Coffee.

Light Colonel
See "Lieutenant Colonel."

Light Duty
Limited duty status due to illness or injury.

Light Duty Chit
Piece of paper which authorizes limited duty due to illness or injury; see "Laminated Light Duty Chit."

Light Up
Fire on a target in combat.

Line
All rope and cord used aboard a ship is called "line."

Line Company
Letter Company; usually refers to infantry companies; companies in a battalion other than H&S.

Line Crossing Ceremony
Held when a ship crosses the equator; King Neptune and his court preside as "Polliwogs" are turned into "Shellbacks."; similar ceremonies are held when a ship crosses other lines.

Lipstick
In the mid-20th Century the lipstick worn by Women Marines was all the same shade – "Montezuma Red"; the color survives in the color of the cord on the female enlisted Marine's garrison cap.

Lipstick Lieutenant
Pejorative term for a Marine warrant officer; so named because the insignia for warrant officers are actually first and second lieutenants' gold and silver bars with stripes of red added; well-liked warrant officers are informally addressed as "Gunner," all others are addressed as "Mister" or "Warrant Officer."

Liquid Asshole
Beer.

Lister Bag
Long canvas bag suspended on a tripod or from a tree limb which contains drinking water; the canvas will "sweat" and provide natural cooling for the water.

LMD
Large Mahogany Desk; used by "Pogues" and "FAGs."

Loader
Tank crewman on a gun tank responsible for operating the .30 cal. machinegun and loading the main cannon.

Salty Language

Lock and Load

Firing line command to load your weapon with ammunition and await further orders from the range officer; in combat it is an informal command to prepare to fight; it can also mean "Pour me a drink" or "Let's do it."

Lock Out

Exit a submarine while submerged; usually done by Recon Marines using SCUBA.

Lock Out a SEAL

Make a bowel movement.

LP

Listening Post; usually set up outside the perimeter at night to provide warning of an enemy attack.

LPC

Leather Personnel Carriers; boots; also called "Cadillacs."

LPD

Landing Platform Dock Assault ship; similar to an "LSD."

LPH

Landing Platform, Helicopter; World War II aircraft carriers converted to accommodate squadrons of Marine helicopters.

LPM

See "Landing Party Manual."

LSD

Landing Ship, Dock; ship designed specifically for amphibious operations; its center is a floodable dock where Marines and their equipment can be loaded into landing craft which can then be floated out the "Stern Gate" and onto the beach.

LST

Landing Ship, Tank; ship designed to run its bow onto a beach; its bow doors open and discharge Marines and their equipment directly into battle; it has a flat bottom, and is no fun to be aboard in rough seas.

Lubriplate®

Commercial lubricant used to protect the wear points of weapons.

Lucy Brewer

Legendary "first" Woman Marine; she supposedly donned men's clothing and found refuge in the Marine Corps during the War of 1812; according to the legend no one discovered she was a woman, and she served as a member of *USS Constitution's* Marine guard and saw action in some of the bloodiest sea fights of the war; the is no way to substantiate her claims, but even so there is a street named in her honor at Camp Lejeune.

Luke the Gook

Viet Cong; cousin of "Link the Chink."

LVS

Logistical Vehicle System; flatbed truck commonly called a "Dragon Wagon."

LVT

Landing Vehicle, Tracked; amphibious tractor; amtrac; floatable armored vehicle which transports Marines from an LST or LPD to and over the beachhead; sometimes called a "Large Vulnerable Target."

LZ

Helicopter Landing Zone; usually designated with a name, i.e. "LZ Lark," "LZ Betty," or "LZ Mouse."

Salty Language

Mike

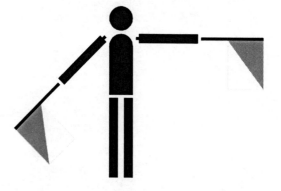

Salty Language

M1

U.S. rifle caliber .30; the primary infantry weapon of World War II and Korea; replaced the Springfield M1903, and was itself replaced by the M14.

M1/M2

.30-cal. carbine rifle.

M2

"Heavy barrel" .50-cal. machinegun developed just after WWI and still being used; nicknamed "Ma-Deuce."

M3A1

.45-cal sub-machinegun known as the "Grease Gun"; a favorite of garrison officers; once the standard on-board weapon for most tank crews.

M9

Beretta 9mm pistol; replaced the M19llA1 .45 in the 1990s.

M14

U.S. rifle, caliber 7.62 mm; designed primarily for semiautomatic fire; infantry weapon in use between Korea and early Vietnam; it replaced the M1, and was itself replaced by the M16.

M16

U.S. rifle, caliber 5.56 mm; a lightweight, air cooled, gas operated, magazine fed, shoulder weapon; capable of both semiautomatic and full automatic fire; basic infantry rifle which replaced the M14 at the start of the Vietnam War; see "Mattel."

M60
Air cooled, belt fed, gas-operated, fully automatic, shoulder-fired standard infantry machinegun 7.62 mm with bipod and replacement barrels.

M249
See "SAW."

M1903
Springfield bolt-action .30 cal rifle; replaced by the M1 in the mid 1930s; the Marine Corps used them through much of World War II.

M1911A1
Automatic pistol, caliber .45; used from World War I until the 1990s; replaced by the M9; usually called a "45."

M1918
Browning Automatic Rifle; known universally as the B.A.R.

Ma-Deuce
M-2 .50-cal machinegun.

Magazine
The component of a rifle which contains ammunition; often called a *clip* in error.

Maggot
One of the lowest forms of life; a favorite DI nickname for recruits; also a Marine who spends most of his or her time trying to obtain a discharge.

MAB
Marine Amphibious Brigade; now called a MEB.

MAC Flight
Low-cost "Space A" flight aboard a military aircraft; can be utilized by active duty personnel, family members and retirees in descending order of preference; still known as a "MAC Flight," despite the redesignation of the "Military Airlift Command"; see "Space A" and "AMC."

MAF
Marine Amphibious Force; now called a "MEF."

MAG
Marine Air Group; unit in an air wing equivalent to an infantry regiment; commanded by a colonel.

MAGTF
Marine Air Ground Task Force; a Marine unit with both air and ground elements.

Maggie's Drawers
Red flag waved from the rifle pits to indicate a complete miss of the target during qualification firing.

Mail Buoy
Non-existent navigational aid used in a practical joke by "salty" Marines and sailors; allegedly the mail buoy or sea buoy is a device to which passing ships would attach packets of mail; "Newbie" Marines or sailors are assigned "Mail Buoy Watch" and told to be on the lookout for one.

Mainside
Main portion of a base or installation where the HQs are located, along with such thing as the Marine Corps Exchange and theater.

Major
Fourth grade of commissioned officer; first of the field grades; indicated by a gold oak leaf on the collar points or epaulets; pay grade is O-4.

Major General
Second of the flag officer ranks; indicated by two silver stars on the collar points or epaulets of the uniform; pay grade is O-8.

Make a Hole
Phrase used to move a group of people not in formation out of the way of a formed unit or a person senior in rank; see "Gangway."

Malingerer
Marine or recruit who spends too much time at sick call or makes other excuses to get out of training or duty; often someone with a "Laminated Light Duty Chit"; malingering is a punishable offense under the UCMJ.

Mameluke Sword
Sword worn by Marine commissioned and warrant officers; The first Mameluke sword was presented to Lieutenant Presley N. O'Bannon by Prince Hamet Bey, the Pasha of Tripoli, in 1805 at which time the United States flag was flown for the first time in the Old World.

Manning the Rails

Done when entering or leaving port, or when rendering special honors; a ship's compliment (including embarked Marines) will turn out in full dress uniforms and stand along the rails or in the rigging at the position of attention.

Manual of Arms

Prescribed movements involving the use of weapons, in particular rifles and swords, in parades and ceremonies.

MarDet

Marine Detachment.

MARG

Mediterranean Amphibious Ready Group; see "ARG."

Marine Band

The United States Marine Band; known as "The President's Own"; located at Marine Barracks 8th and I, Washington, DC; the official band of the Marine Corps; other bands exist at division, air wing and depot levels throughout the Marine Corps.

Marine Barracks

Marine Corps posts around the world which provide security for naval and other government installations.

Marine Brat

See "Military Brat."

Marine Combat Training (MCT)
Infantry training provided to every Marine not assigned an Infantry MOS; see "School of Infantry."

Marine Corps Association (MCA)
Formed at Guantanamo Bay, Cuba on 25 April 1913, by Marines of the Second Provisional Brigade; John A. Lejeune, then a lieutenant colonel, headed its first executive committee; the purpose of the MCA is to disseminate knowledge of the military art amongst its members.

Marine Corps Birthday Ball
Any event from a buffet dinner to a "Mess Night" held on or close to November 10th each year to commemorate the birthday of the United States Marine Corps in 1775; to qualify as such, it must have a decorated cake so that the first two pieces can go to the oldest and youngest Marines present; the Commandant's Birthday Order and the Birthday Message of Major General Commandant John A. Lejeune must also be read.

Marine Corps Exchange (MCX)
The correct name of the "PX"; on Navy bases you will find a Navy Exchange (NEX), and on Army and Air Force installations they will have an Army and Air Force Exchange Service (AAFES); abbreviated "MCX."

Marine Corps Gazette
The magazine for professional Marines; published by the Marine Corps Association.

Marine Corps Hymn
DOES NOT EXIST; see "Marines' Hymn."

Marine Corps League (MCL)
National organization of Marines and former Marines; it has local detachments throughout the country.

Marine Corps War Memorial
Proper name for the "Iwo Jima Statue" located near Arlington National Cemetery in Washington D.C.

Marine Detachment
Small unit of Marines assigned as part of a ship's compliment to provide guards, operate the brig, provide orderlies to senior Navy officers, and man one or more of the naval guns; see "Seagoing Marine."

Marine Expeditionary Brigade (MEB)
Consists of a Regimental Landing Team, Marine Air Group, and a Brigade Service Support Group; commanded by a brigadier general; it is a self-sufficient fighting element; formerly a "MAB."

Marine Expeditionary Force (MEF)
Built around a complete "Division-Wing Team" with combat support and combat service support groups; a MEF consists of about 53,000 Marines and sailors.

Marine Expeditionary Unit (MEU)
Smallest of the expeditionary organizations; built around a Battalion Landing Team and a Composite Air Squadron; consists of approximately 2,500 Marines.

Marine Regs
Term used in the Navy to refer to Navy medical or dental personnel who opt to wear Marine Corps uniforms while serving with the "FMF"; sailors who choose to do this agree to meet Marine Corps uniform regulations, including grooming and physical standards.

Marine House
Used often on embassy (MSG) duty to designate the residence of Marines in a civilian neighborhood or on the grounds of an embassy overseas; sometimes used for any free-standing barracks for Marines.

Marines' Hymn
Official song of the United States Marine Corps; when it is played all Marines (including "former" Marines) stand at attention and face the music; it is *not* called the "Marine Corps Hymn!"

Marine One
Call sign of Marine aircraft in which the President of the United States is either passenger or pilot; usually one of the specially built helicopters assigned to "HMX-1" for Presidential Support; most often used to transport the President from the White House lawn to Air Force One or Camp David, MD.

Marking Time
Marching in place; also to wait around; kill time.

MARTD
Marine Air Reserve Training Detachment

Massaro, John E.
Eighth Sergeant Major of the Marine Corps; served from April 1, 1977 through Aug. 15, 1979.

Master at Arms
Ship's policeman; usually a senior petty officer charged with keeping order aboard ship or in a Navy organization; sometimes they call upon Marines to assist in their duties.

Master Gunnery Sergeant of Marines
The senior enlisted technician in any MOS; insignia is three chevrons and four rockers with a bursting bomb between chevrons and rockers; pay grade is E-9 (same as a sergeant major); sometimes called "Master Guns."

Master Guns
See "Master Gunnery Sergeant of Marines."

Master Sergeant
Army and Air Force enlisted ranks; see "Master Sergeant of Marines."

Master Sergeant of Marines
Three chevrons and three rockers with crossed rifles between chevrons and rockers; pay grade is E-8 (the same as a first sergeant); sometimes called "Top."

Mattel
Toy company erroneously reported to have been the original manufacturer of the M16 rifle; the rifle was detested by our troops at the start of the Vietnam war

because it was prone to sand and dirt-induced jams, and the stocks broke with very little impact; replaced by the M16A3; see "M16."

Mattress
A prostitute or other person who spends a lot of time in the prone or supine position giving sexual gratification to Marines.

Mattress Pressing
Sleeping.

MAU
Marine Amphibious Unit; now called a "MEU."

MAW
Marine Air Wing; equivalent to an infantry division; commanded by a major general.

MCAS
Marine Corps Air Station.

MCB
Marine Corps Base.

MCBH
Marine Corps Base Hawaii.

McCawley, Charles
Eighth Commandant of the Marine Corps; named Colonel Commandant on the resignation of Brigadier General Jacob Zeilin on Oct. 31, 1876; the law making the Commandant a brigadier general had been repealed during Zeilin's term; McCawley resigned Jan. 29, 1891.

McHugh, Thomas J.
Third Sergeant Major of the Marine Corps; served from June 29, 1962 until July 16, 1965.

MCI
Marine Corps Institute; correspondence school for Marine Corps leadership and technical training.

McKeon, Matthew
Infamous Staff Sergeant of Marines; see "Ribbon Creek."

MCLB
Marine Corps Logistics Bases; located at Albany, GA and Barstow, CA.

McMichael, Alford L.
Fourteenth Sergeant Major of the Marine Corps; the first "Dark Green Marine" to serve in that position; served from July 1, 1999 to June 26, 2003.

MCRD
Marine Corps Recruit Depot; there are two, one is at Parris Island, S.C. and the other is located in San Diego, CA.; see "Hollywood Marines."

MCT
Marine Combat Training; infantry training provided to every Marine not assigned an Infantry MOS.

MCX
Marine Corps Exchange.

Meat Wagon
Ambulance; mainly used when one is standing by during close combat training, or is following a unit on a "hump."

MEB
Marine Expeditionary Brigade; formerly a "MAB."

MECEP
Marine Enlisted Commissioning Education Program; program which provides outstanding enlisted Marines the opportunity to become Marine Corps officers; Marines successfully completing the program receive a Baccalaureate Degree and a commission as a second lieutenant.

Medal of Honor
The nation's highest award for bravery; it is *not* called the Congressional Medal of Honor; more correctly, it is the Army, Navy or Air Force Medal of Honor.

Medevac
Medical Evacuation of wounded, usually by helicopter; first used during the Korean War, and perfected in Vietnam; now a standard medical term used worldwide.

Medical Battalion
A predominantly Navy medical unit in an FSSG which provides additional support to Marine operational units in the field and units which do not have corpsmen assigned to them.

MEF
Marine Expeditionary Force.

MER
Maximum Effective Range; the distance at which a weapon system can be expected to regularly hit a target.

Meritorious Mast
Formation during which awards and promotions are made; from navy tradition of gathering the crew around the main mast of a ship to deliver punishments and rewards; in the modern Marine Corps, it is a written recognition of work well done, and is of greater value than a Letter of Appreciation.

Meritorious Promotion
Promotion given to a Marine as a result of outstanding performance of duty; usually the result of competition in a "Meritorious Promotion Board"; see also "Hip Pocket Promotion."

Mess Deck
Dining room aboard ship; from the naval term.

Mess Hall
Dining Facility.

Mess Night
Formal dinner and ceremony having strict rules, toasts and responses; the uniform is always evening dress unless the unit is in a forward area, where the appropriate field uniform is acceptable (in which case it is called a "Field Mess"); a unique evening of fraternity open only to Marines or specifically invited guests (spouses are seldom, if ever allowed to

attend); separate events are often held for Commissioned and Warrant Officers, Staff Non-commissioned Officers, and Non-commissioned officers; sometimes they are open to all ranks; see "Dining In."

MEU
Marine Expeditionary Unit; smallest of the expeditionary organizations; built around a Battalion Landing Team and a Composite Air Squadron; consists of approximately 2,500 Marines (Pronounced *mew*).

MFF
Military Freefall; parachuting without use of a "Static Line"; it is a high-altitude special operations insertion technique; also called "HALO."

MFICC
Mother Fucker In Complete Charge; another version of "HMFIC."

MIA
Missing In Action.

Mickey Mouse Boots
Cold weather boots worn by Marines; so named because they are huge, like Mickey's feet; proper name is "VB" or "Vapor Barrier" boots.

Midrats
Midnight Rations; food served from midnight to reveille for those getting off or going on duty during the middle of the night.

Midshipman
Student at the U. S. Naval Academy; prior to the establishment of the Naval Academy in 1847 it was an entry-level rank to commissioning as a Naval officer; a certain percentage of each class are commissioned as Marine officers upon graduation; the Naval Academy football team is called the "Midshipmen."

Midwatch
Guard post or duty from midnight until 0400; see "Watch."

Mighty Mite
Small Jeep-like vehicle made specifically for the Marine Corps by American Motors Corporation during the Vietnam War.

Mike Boat
Generic name used for any landing craft with a bow ramp.

Mike Mike
Millimeter.

Mikes
Minutes or millimeters, as appropriate.

MILES
Multiple Integrated Laser Engagement System; consists of a vest containing sensors, and a laser designator which attaches to the barrel of a rifle; allows "TECG" to determine who has been "shot" during combat training exercises; MILES gear was used in the movie "Heartbreak Ridge."

Military Brat
The child of someone in the military; originally a put-down, it is now a term embraced by most Military Brats; they take pride in the informal education which living with their military dad or mom (or both) in a variety of unique places has afforded them.

Military Creases
Vertical creases ironed into a uniform shirt - two on the front running through the shirt pocket buttons, and three evenly spaced on the back; some Army and Air Force types have them sewn in, while Marines always *iron* them in.

Military Occupational Specialty (MOS)
The job specialty of a Marine; a specific job in a broader "Occupational Field."

Miller, Samuel
Adjutant and Inspector of the Marine Corps and a Brevet Major, he served as Acting Commandant of the Marine Corps from the 2nd to the 15th of Sept. 1818; replaced as Acting Commandant by Brevet Major Archibald Henderson on Sept 16, 1818.

Miramar
MCAS in southern California; home of the 3rd Marine Air Wing, which was formerly based at the now closed MCAS at El Toro.

Missing Man Formation
A flight of aircraft (usually five) in a fly-over formation; when the flight reaches the honor point,

one of the aircraft peels off into a steep climb, leaving his position vacant; a formal salute rendered to POWs and MIAs, as well as to deceased military people - usually aviators.

Mister Vice
Junior officer or NCO at a Mess Night; responsible for organizing the entire evening; sits alone at his own table; grants or denies members of the Mess access to the President; collects and accounts for "fines."

Mk19 Mod 3
40-mm machinegun-type grenade launcher.

M-NU
Fluid used by Marines to renew emblems and metal rank insignia which are showing metal through the black coloring; originally dark brown, since Marine Corps emblems were that color until about 1960 when emblems and shoes became black; the name stands for eMblem-reNU.

Mo Skosh
Very small; see "Skoshi."

MO
Medical Officer; a Navy doctor.

MOH
Medal of Honor; highest military award for valor; there are three separate designs: Army, Navy and Air Force; the criteria is the same for all; it is *not* called the *Congressional* Medal of Honor!

MOJO
> Originally a concoction of hard liquors designed for the sole purpose of getting drunk; also used to mean a swaggering approach or a smooth talking individual, as in "He's got his MOJO going."

MOLLE
> Modular Lightweight Load Carrying Equipment; a system which replaced the traditional harness, belt and pack system in order to allow a Marine to "wear" rather than "carry" his equipment.

Molly Marine
> Statue of a Woman Marine located in New Orleans, LA; the first statue of a woman in military service in the United States.

Montford Point
> Section of Camp Lejeune, N.C. at which "Dark Green" Marines were trained during World War II; prior to that time there *were* no black Marines.

Montezuma Red
> Crimson color of the Blood Stripe on dress uniform of Marine commissioned and noncommissioned officers; also the color of lipstick worn by early Women Marines.

Moonbeam
> Flashlight.

MOPP
> Military Oriented Protective Posture; the four levels of protection against an "NBC" attack.

Salty Language

Mortar
> Indirect fire weapon; fires a projectile in a high arch to reach an impact point.

MOS
> Military Occupational Specialty; each is identified by a 4-digit code; the first two numbers denote the "OF," and the second two identify a specific job within it; see "OF."

Motivational Platoon
> Special platoon where "problem recruits" were once sent; its members spent the day crawling through sewage, busting rocks, and engaging in "Incentive PT"; borderline recruits were sent to "One Day Moto," and "hard cases" went to "One *Week* Moto"; most of those sent there were model recruits once they returned to their training platoon, since "regular boot camp" was a breeze in comparison; discontinued (unfortunately) due to Congressional whining.

Moto Platoon
> See "Motivational Platoon."

Motor T
> Motor Transport; their motto is, "We may not be the pride, but without *us* the pride don't ride!"

Mount Up
> Cavalry term meaning to mount your horse and prepare to move out; in the infantry it means to put on your pack and get ready to move out.

MOUT
> Military Operations is Urban Terrain; a MOUT facility is a replica town built aboard Marine Corps bases in order to give Marines a place to practice "house to house fighting"; often called "Combat Town."

MP
> Military Police; at one time an additional duty; now a professional MOS with both guard and law enforcement responsibilities; many Marines swear it *really* stands for "Military Prick."

MPC
> Military Pay Certificates; scrip issued instead of dollars by Marines in Japan (following WWII) and Vietnam (during that conflict) to discourage black marketeering.

Mr. Charles
> Vietnamese Communist soldier; usually called "Charlie."

MRE
> Meal, Ready to Eat; standard field rations which come in a plastic pouch and are sometimes dehydrated; often called "Meal that Refuses to Exit," or "Meals Rejected by Ethiopians"; replaced "C-Rations."

MSG
> Marine Security Guard; see "Embassy Marine."

MSPF

Maritime Special Purpose Force; specialized sub-unit of a MEU(SOC); provides an enhanced operational capability to execute selected maritime special missions; the primary components are a Force Recon Detachment and a SEAL platoon.

MSSG

MEU Service Support Group; the Combat Service Support Element of a MEU.

MTT

Mobile Training Team; a traveling "schoolhouse" used to take training to Marine units rather than vice versa.

Mud Marines

Term used by Marine aviation personnel when referring to infantry Marines.

Mule

Little more than a platform on wheels, with a two-cylinder Tecumseh engine started with a pull-cord just like a power lawnmower; it had four-wheel drive and steering; it could carry literally a ton of supplies, or be mounted with M60 mortars, small cannon or the 105mm recoilless rifle; retired due to the faulty design of the tires and lack of protection for the driver.

Multi-fueler

Vehicle designed to use multiple types of fuel including gasoline, diesel or jet fuel.

Mundy Jr., Carl E.
Thirtieth Commandant of the Marine Corps; served from July 1, 1991 until June 30, 1995.

Mustang
Commissioned officer who served previously as an enlisted person.

MWTC
Marine Corps Mountain Warfare Training Center; located at Pickel Meadows in the Sierra Nevada Mountains;   also called "Bridgeport."

November

Napalm
Highly volatile gasoline in a jelly form used for burning out caves during World War II; dropped from aircraft in canisters to great effect in Vietnam.

Nape
(*n*) Napalm; (*v*) to drop napalm on a target.

NAS
Naval Air Station.

Navajo Code Talkers
See "Code Talkers."

Naval Gunfire (NGF)
Artillery support from ships at sea; not useful against targets in defilade (on the reverse slope of a hill) because of flat trajectory; guns are actually called "Naval Rifles."

Navy Construction Battalion
Combat engineers and construction forces better known as "Seabees."

Navy Shower
Type of shower taken while a ship is at sea to conserve fresh water; the individual lathers up completely with the water turned off, and then rinses off the soap as quickly as possible; another type of "Navy Shower" is when someone skips showering altogether, and instead puts on a clean pair of skivvies and some deodorant.

NBC

Nuclear, Biological and Chemical; see "Gas Chamber."

NCIS

Naval Criminal Investigation Service; detective force for the naval services; consists of commissioned, warrant and non-commissioned officers, as well as civilians; they wear civilian clothing, and are given the rank of "Special Agent."

NCO

Noncommissioned officer; all ranks (except lance corporal) containing the word corporal or sergeant; they are: corporal, sergeant, staff sergeant, gunnery sergeant, master sergeant, first sergeant, sergeant major, master gunnery sergeant and Sergeant Major of the Marine Corps.

NCOIC

Noncommissioned officer in charge; the senior enlisted Marine in detachments and guard units, particularly when there is no commissioned officer assigned.

Near Beer

Low alcohol-content beer given out at unit events.

Negligent Discharge

The unintentional firing of a weapon; formerly known as an "Accidental Discharge" or "AD."

NEO
> Noncombatant Evacuation Operation; essentially a rescue mission for civilians caught up in dangerous situations overseas.

New River
> MCAS (Helicopter) adjacent to CLNC.

Neville, Wendell
> Fourteenth Commandant of the Marine Corps; recipient of the Medal of Honor; appointed Major General Commandant on March 5, 1929 and died in office.

Newbie
> New member of a unit, usually one with little military experience who is the object of numerous practical jokes; one usually *remains* a newbie until the *next* newbie comes aboard; see "FNG."

NFG
> No Fucking Good.

NGF
> Naval Gunfire.

Nicholas, Samuel
> First "Commandant" of the Marine Corps; commissioned a "Captain of Marines" by the Continental Congress on Nov. 28, 1775 and promoted to major on June 25, 1776; while the resolution of Congress on Nov. 10, 1775 provided for a colonel to command two battalions of Marines,

Nicholas was the senior officer when the organization ceased to exist in 1781 and is therefore considered to be the first Commandant.

Nicholson, Augustus S.

Acting Commandant from May 13 until June 9, 1864; Major, Adjutant and Inspector of the Corps; served between the death of Harris and the appointment of Zeilin.

Nine Yards

As used in, "The Whole Nine Yards"; refers to a complete belt of machinegun ammo, which is 27 feet long.

NJP

Non-judicial punishment; article 15 of the UCMJ.

Noncommissioned Officer

See "NCO."

Noncommissioned Officer Sword

The 1859 Field and Staff Officer sword; badge of office carried on parade or in formal situations by NCOs; the Marine Corps is the only service which allows NCOs to carry a sword.

Non-judicial Punishment (NJP)

Article 15 of the UCMJ; punishment under which does not require a court martial; for minor infractions; usually administered by the Marine's commanding officer or a ship's captain.

Non-qual

A Marine who did not qualify as an expert, sharpshooter or marksman on the rifle range; non-quals do not graduate from boot camp; also called an "Unq" (Unqualified).

Noted

Answer meaning "understood" when receiving a list of instructions; also an indication that something was written down.

NP Mat

Neoprene Mat; sealed cell sleeping mat which contains no neoprene and keeps dampness from permeating your sleeping bag; the modern version is the "Isopor" mat; see "Pussy Pad."

Number One

The best.

Number Ten

The worst.

Numbnuts

Ignorant or untrainable; used often by drill instructors to describe recruits.

NVA

North Vietnamese Army.

Salty Language

Oscar

Salty Language

O'Bannon, Presley N.
Famous Lieutenant of Marines; see "Mameluke Sword."

Obstacle Course
Series of physical barriers which a Marine must navigate in a race against time; see "Confidence Course."

Oceanside
Civilian community outside the main gate of Camp Pendleton, CA; sometimes called "Oceanslime."

O-Club
Officer's Club; place where "Zeros" gather to "Splice the Main Brace."

O-Course
Obstacle Course.

OCS
Officer Candidates School.

OD
Olive drab; official color of utility and fatigue uniforms worn prior to the introduction of cammies; the term was replaced by "Sage Green," and then simply "Green"; also commonly used in reference to the "OOD."

OF
Occupational Field; it is indicated by a two-digit designation; examples are "Communications" (25) and "Infantry" (03); OFs are further subdivided into specific MOSs; see "MOS."

Office Hours

Non-judicial hearing for minor offences at which NJP (non-judicial punishment) may be issued by a commanding officer; also called "Article 15," which is the section of the UCMJ it falls under.

Office Pogue

Office clerk; see "Remington Raider" and "Ball Bearing BAM."

Officer

General use refers to commissioned officers and warrant officers; noncommissioned officers are *also* officers, but are generally referred to as NCOs.

Officers' Country

Area aboard ship where commissioned officer living compartments are located; off-limits to all enlisted personnel unless they are on official duty.

Officer Candidates School (OCS)

Training program for motivated college graduates who have been screened by the Marine Corps for the qualities necessary to become a leader of Marines; upon graduation they are commissioned as Second Lieutenants of Marines.

Oh Dark Thirty

See "Zero Dark Thirty."

OIC

Officer in Charge; commissioned or warrant officer placed in charge of a group of Marines or a project; this person is not a commander, and does not have the UCMJ authority vested in a commander.

OIF

Operation Iraqi Freedom; sometimes called the "Second Gulf War."

OIF II

Operation Iraqi Freedom II; the Iraqi War after "the end of major hostilities."

OJT

On the Job Training; some MOSs may be acquired by this method, rather than by attending a formal school.

Oki

Okinawa; island south of Japan owned by the U. S. Government until the 1970s when it was returned to Japan; still a major Marine Corps installation, it was used during Vietnam as a staging point for troops going into and out of that country; currently home to the bulk of the 3rd Marine Division; best known to Marines as "The Rock."

Old Corps

The Marine Corps you belonged to five minutes before the guy you are talking to joined; "salts" always wax nostalgic about the "Old Corps"; also used in reference to how a Marine does something, i.e. "That was *Old* Corps!"

Old Hat

Stale or unchanged information; information which is already known.

Old Man
Commanding Officer; used informally between "snuffies."

On Station
Usually refers to a ship or aircraft being at its assigned position; also sometimes used to mean "on duty."

On the Beach
Ashore; on liberty.

Ontos
Vietnam-era fighting vehicle which looked like a small tank with six externally mounted 105mm recoilless rifles attached; ammunition and a loader were carried inside, but he had to get out to load the tubes; when all six rifles were fired at the same time, the Ontos would stand up on its hind section; it was a great weapon to use as part of the "FPF"; the name is Greek for "thing."

OOD
Officer of the Day; aboard ship, the "Officer of the Deck."

Oooh-Raah
Sound made by a Marine to indicate agreement, approval, or provide encouragement.

OP
Observation Post.

OPSEC
Operational Security; hush-hush; when you can't or won't talk about something, it is said to be "Opsec."

Op Tempo
Operational Tempo; how frequently a unit deploys or goes to the field.

OQR
Officer Qualification Record; similar to the enlisted "SRB."

Order of the Golden Dragon
Awarded for crossing the International Date Line; see "Line Crossing Ceremony."

Orderly Sergeant
Highest enlisted rank in the Marine Corps during the Civil War; most ships' Marine Detachments were commanded by Orderly Sergeants; not presently in use.

Oscar
Name of the dummy used for "man overboard" drills; also the flag which is hoisted when there is a man overboard (the flag for the letter "O").

Oscar Mike
On the Move.

OSCD
Overseas Control Date; the date a Marine's last extended overseas tour concluded; used to determine when his *next* one will *begin*.

OSO
Officer Selection Officer.

Osprey
V-22 tilt-wing VSTOL aircraft; will replace the aging fleet of CH-46 helicopters.

Out
I am finished talking, and do not expect or require a reply from you; thus, "over and out" is a self-contradiction.

Outfuckingstanding
Marine expletive meaning "very, very good."

OV-10
Bronco observation aircraft; acted as a "FAC aloft" to direct air strikes; no longer in service.

Over
I am finished talking, and now expect *you* to talk.

Over and Out
Does not exist except in the movies; an oxymoron.

Over the Hill
Unauthorized Absence.

Overhead
Ceiling; from the naval term.

Overstreat, Harold G.
Twelfth Sergeant Major of the Marine Corps; served from June 28, 1991 until June 29, 1995.

Papa

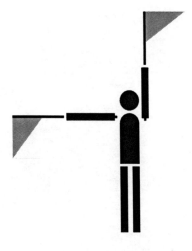

Salty Language

P-38

Tool contained in every case of C-Rations; used primarily as a can opener; so versatile Marines used it as a Phillips and slot screw driver, rudimentary box opener, scraper and even push tool; generally worn on the "Dog Tag" chain around the neck; also called a "John Wayne."

Page 11

Page in the service record book containing a chronological listing of favorable and unfavorable actions; entries can range from listing a DUI, to warnings about the length of the grass at your assigned quarters; positive entries include everything from a thank you letter from a community agency, to a Medal of Honor; even so, it is usually a bad thing when a Marine is told, "You are going to get a Page 11 for that!"

Panther Piss

Cheap beer; see "Near Beer."

Pappy Boyington

Colonel Gregory "Pappy" Boyington; Medal of Honor recipient, Commanding Officer of the famed "Black Sheep" during WWII; called "Pappy" or "Gramps" because he was much older than the other pilots (he was thirty-one years old at the time).

Parade Deck

See "Grinder."

Parkerize™
Chemical process using phosphorus to put a strong coating on a weapon; considered far superior to "bluing."

Parris Island SC (PISC)
Location of the Marine Corps' east coast Recruit Depot; named for its previous owner, it has been a naval facility since the Civil War and a Marine Corps activity since 1915; the only training site for female Marines; often known simply as "PI" or "The Island."

Passageway
Hallway or corridor; from the naval usage.

Passed Over
Eligible and considered, but not selected, for promotion.

Password
Pre-determined word or phrase which is given in response to the challenge of a sentry; literally, a word needed in order to pass.

Pate, Randolph McCall
Twenty-first Commandant of the Marine Corps; served as Commandant from Jan. 1, 1956 until Dec. 31, 1959.

Pay Grade
A relational term consisting of the letter E, O or W and the level of pay assigned to that grade.

PC

Politically Correct; i.e. the next entry is *not*.

PCFSMFSOB

Piss, cunt, fuck, shit, motherfucker, son of a bitch!; an expletive said quickly while angry or in pain.

PCP

Physical Conditioning Platoon; special unit in boot camp to which recruits unable to maintain minimal physical conditioning are sent; their entire day is spent in physical conditioning, and once they meet the standard they are placed back into training with a platoon which is at the point where they were removed from the cycle; often called "Pork Chop Platoon."

PCS

Permanent Change of Station; leaving one unit to be assigned to another; generally involves travel pay, household goods shipments, and a total disruption of life.

PCSO

Permanent Change of Station Orders.

PEBD

Pay Entry Base Date; the date from which pay longevity is computed; usually the first enlistment or commissioning date.

Pecker Checker

Navy Corpsman; came into vogue during the days of the "Short Arm Inspection."

Pelicans
Navy pilots.

Pencil Whip
Intentionally falsify logs or records by filling in the blanks just before an inspection.

Permanent Party
Person assigned to a base, station or ship on Permanent Change of Station orders, as opposed to someone assigned temporarily.

Permissive TAD
Permissive Temporary Duty; granted for temporary duty away from the normal assigned duties; no additional pay is given; for example, PTAD is granted for "recruiter assistance" duty.

Petty Officer
A Navy and Coast Guard series of ranks vaguely equivalent to noncommissioned officers; the insignia consists of from one to three inverted chevrons with a Navy Eagle (called a "crow") perched on top; between the eagle and the chevrons is a graphic which indicates the specialty of that particular petty officer.

PF
Popular Forces; Vietnam's "National Guard" - farmers during the day, and soldiers at night; usually untrained and dangerous.

PFC
Private First Class; pay grade E-2; also "Private Fucking Citizen" (see "CivDiv")

PFT
Physical Fitness Test; biannual test to ensure Marines are within Marine Corps standards; includes a timed three-mile run, pull-ups (for men) or bent arm hang (for women), and crunches; a perfect score (called "maxing the PFT," and seldom attained) is 300; the Marine's height to weight ratio is also measured, and must fall within established standards.

Phantom
Nickname of the F-4B jet fighter/bomber aircraft flown by Marines in Vietnam.

Pharmacist Mate
Navy Corpsman rank in WWII and Korea; see Corpsman."

Philippine Haircut
A slit throat.

Phrog
See "Frog."

PI
Parris Island.

PI, The
The Philippine Islands.

Pie Hole
Mouth; also "Cake Hole" and "Soup Cooler."

Pig Board
Bulletin board set up in a common area (mostly in boot camp) to which photos of wives and girlfriends are posted; sometimes awards are given for "quality" posts; also called a "Hog Board."

Pinning On
Tradition among enlisted Marines in which anyone senior in rank to a newly promoted Marine is allowed to punch the new rank insignia, thereby "pinning them on"; also called "Tacking On"; it is also a custom for Recon Marines to have their gold jump wings literally pinned into their naked chests; the practice was outlawed, but some Marines still have it done in private; see "Blood Wings" and "Gold Wing Ceremony."

PISC
Parris Island, South Carolina.

Piss 'n Puke
Confinement to the brig on bread and water while aboard ship; also called "Piss 'n Punk."

Pisscutter
Garrison cover; sometimes "pisscover"; the WM version is a "cunt cap."

Pissing Contest
An argument, usually without purpose or value.

Piss Test
Urinalysis.

Pith Helmet
Khaki colored fiber helmet used extensively for the jungle environment; worn by Marines throughout the 20th Century in boot camp, in war, and in the fleet; presently worn by primary marksmanship instructors.

Pitting
To pit; a boot camp verb meaning to give "Incentive Training" (IT) to a recruit in order to improve his or her motivation, or as punishment for a minor infraction of rules; sand pits are located throughout the MCRDs for this purpose; see also "Quarterdecking."

Pits
Area behind the mound on a firing range where targets are pulled, marked and repaired before being hoisted to be fired upon again; often called the "Butts."

Pizza Box
See "Toilet Seat."

Platoon
Sub-unit within a company; consisting of four squads in the infantry; usually commanded by a lieutenant; the basic working unit in boot camp, where its leaders are drill instructors.

Plank Owner
Part of something new; usually refers to the original crew members of a newly commissioned ship.

PLC
Platoon Leaders' Course; an innovative officer training program in which participants take part in officer training during the summers of their college years; upon graduation from college these individuals are commissioned as Second Lieutenants of Marines; there are no classes or commitments during the school year; the program has two career specific tracks - aviation and legal.

PLF
Parachute Landing Fall.

PM
Preventive Maintenance; first level (echelon) maintenance of vehicles and equipment.

PME
Professional Military Education; can be resident (i.e. the SNCO Academy) or non-resident (through MCI courses); completion of the non-resident course appropriate to a Marine's grade is required for promotion; that is not the case with resident courses, since all Marines do not have the same opportunity to attend due to remote duty assignments.

PMI
Primary Marksmanship Instructor; the "Hat" who "teaches a boot to shoot."

PMO
Provost Marshal's Office; the military police.

Pocket Promotion
See "Hip Pocket Promotion."

Podunk
Any small town; someone's hometown, unless they are from a big city.

Pogey Bait
Candy or other junk food; see "Geedunk."

Pogey Bait 6th
A pejorative term for the Sixth Marine Regiment; according to legend the 6th Marines once sailed aboard a ship which carries tons of candy bars, and only one bar of soap; see "French Fourragere."

Pogey Rope
A pejorative term for the "French Fourragere."

Pogue
Headquarters or office person with no understanding of the *real* Marine Corps; a "REMF."

Point
Lead Marine in a patrol, or lead element in a company; also anyone who takes the lead in performing some task.

Police
To clean up or pick up trash in an area, such as policing the firing line for brass.

Police Call
When every swinging dick gets on line to police the area; "If it doesn't grow, pick it up!"

Police Flag
Sometimes called the "Distress Flag"; the national flag flown upside down; only used when an extreme situation confronts the captain of a ship; never used ashore.

Police Sergeant
NCO charged with barracks maintenance.

Police Shed
Where maintenance tools and linen for the barracks are stored; where the "Police Sergeant" can be found.

Pollywog
Someone one who has never crossed the equator while aboard ship, and/or has not been initiated into the "Realm of Neptune"; see "Shellback."

Poncho
Multi-purpose rectangle of rubberized canvas with a hole (and hood) in the middle so the head can be inserted; used to fend off rain, construct a makeshift tent, or carry bodies, among other things.

Poncho Liner
Camouflaged, quilted, lightweight nylon blanket which ties to the inside of a poncho; usually the only blanket carried by troops in Vietnam.

Pop Smoke

Mark an HLZ with a smoke grenade; also, to leave a location.

Portholes

Eyeglasses; windows; also holes in the sides of a ship used to provide light and sometimes ventilation.

Poolee

Unofficial rank assigned by Marine recruiters to newly enlisted recruits in the Delayed Entry Program who are awaiting departure for recruit training; some recruiters have regular, mandatory formations in which rudimentary drill and physical training are conducted.

Poop

Information; as in "straight poop," "bad poop" or "poop from the group."

Pop Ups

Aluminum hand-held tubes holding a flare attached to a small parachute for field illumination.

Pork Chop Platoon

See "PCP."

Port

Left; from the naval term; originally "Larboard"; changed in the late 18th Century to keep it from being confused with "Starboard," which means right; the port side of a ship is illuminated with a red light.

Port and Starboard Liberty
Situation where half of a unit is always on duty, while the other half is on liberty.

POS
Piece of Shit.

Pos
Location of a friendly; short for "Position" (Pronounced *poz*)

Poser
Someone who "talks the talk," but doesn't "walk the walk"; can be a civilian who says he is a Marine, a mess cook who says he is in Force Recon, or a "REMF" who claims to be a combat vet.

PosRep
Position Report.

Post
(*n*) place where a Marine is assigned, such as a sentry post or an embassy; used extensively by the Army to designate bases not named forts; (*v*) a command in marching for specific officers to take their assigned positions; also the act of placing a sentry on post, or assigning a Marine to a duty station.

Postbox Rear Admiral
See "Tombstone Brigadier General."

Post One

Primary MSG Post at the front entrance to an embassy or consulate, the Marine manning it controls access through the "hard line," monitors closed circuit cameras, and acts as a security focal point.

POTUS

President of the United States; originally used by the Secret Service; the phrase was picked up by Department of Defense and other government agencies in the 1990s.

Pounding your pud

Standing around doing nothing; wasting time; derived from a colloquial expression for masturbating.

POV

Privately Owned Vehicle.

POW

Prisoner of War; see "EPW."

PRC

Portable Radio Communications (Pronounced *prick*)

Precedence

Formal list of commissioned officers in the Naval Service and their position of authority relative to each other; also the priority with which a message must be delivered; the four levels of precedence are Routine, Priority, Immediate and Flash.

President's Own
Name given to the United States Marine Corps Band; the official band of the President of the United States.

Prick (PRC)
Radio Set; in Vietnam it was usually the AN/PRC-25, but it now the PRC-77 or PRC-119.

Prime Mover
Truck.

Private
First enlisted rank in the Marine Corps; identified by having no insignia of rank; pay grade is E-1; sometimes called a "Slick Sleeve."

Private First Class
Second enlisted rank in the Marine Corps; designated by a single chevron on each sleeve or collar; pay grade is E-2; commonly called a "PFC."

Promotion Board
See "Selection Board."

Pros and Cons
Proficiency and conduct marks; given to Marines below the rank of sergeant by their supervisors; used as part of the formula for promotion; each is between 0 (totally unsat, probably not breathing) and 5 (walks on water).

Provost Marshal
Officer in charge of the military police.

PT
Physical Training.

PT Gear
Clothing worn for "PT"; a prescribed uniform usually consisting of t-shirt and shorts, or sweats; usually green on green, unless a unit t-shirt has been authorized.

PTSD
Post-Traumatic Stress Disorder; previously called "Shell Shock" (WWI) and "Battle Fatigue" (WWII); often manifests as dreams recalling battlefield situations, or as a response to loud or sharp sounds.

Pucker Factor
Measure of the stress level in any situation, but especially a dangerous one; a high pucker factor means high stress.

Pucket, Clinton A.
Sixth Sergeant Major of the Marine Corps; served in that position from Feb 1, 1973 through May 31, 1975.

Puff the Magic Dragon
C-47 cargo aircraft converted into a gunship by the addition of several mini-guns.

Pugil Sticks
Padded training sticks used to simulate bayonet fighting.

Pull Butts
The act of marking and scoring targets on the rifle range.

Puller, Lewis B.
See "Chesty."

Pump
Deployment cycle; usually lasts 6 months.

Pump Bilges
Use the "Head"; urinate.

Punji Sticks
Bamboo sticks sharpened and often laced with poison; placed in holes and covered so that a Marine would step in and impale himself; also called "Punji Stakes."

Punch Out
Eject from an aircraft in distress; leave a location.

Pussy Pad
Sleeping mat; see "NP Mat."

Pussy Patch
Medicated patch given to those who get seasick.

Puzzle Palace
Specifically the Pentagon; can be any headquarters.

PX
Post Exchange; Army term; see "Marine Corps Exchange."

Quebec

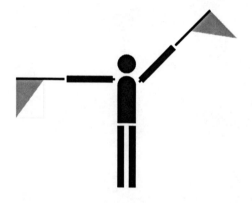

Salty Language

Salty Language

Q-Hut
See "Quonset Hut."

Q-Town
Quaint little town within the confines of MCB Quantico, VA.

Quad 50s
Four .50-cal machineguns mounted in tandem.

Quantico
Marine Corps Base south of Washington, D.C.; home of the Marine Corps University and most training for commissioned officers; also headquarters of the Marine Corps Association; nicknamed the "Crossroads of the Marine Corps."

Quarterdeck
Location of the "Officer of the Deck" aboard ship; the ceremonial seat of authority in any shore-based unit; where one goes to report in to a new command; the section of a recruit squad bay set aside for physical punishment of errant recruits.

Quarterdecking
To be taken to the quarterdeck for "Incentive Training" by a drill instructor; outdoors it is called "Pitting."

Quartermaster Sergeant
Second ranking enlisted grade in the Marine Corps during the Civil War; not presently used.

Quarters
Living space; can be a house, or a barracks.

Quatrefoil
Four-pointed decoration on the top of a warrant or commissioned officer's dress and service caps; according to tradition the design was first used on sailing ships so that Marine sharpshooters in the rigging could identify (and therefore not shoot) their own officers on deck.

Quick Time
Normal pace in marching; approximately 120 steps per minute.

Quit
The "Q" word; not used by Marines; this word has no place in the Corps; see "Fail"; (the one exception is when a Marine is reciting his 5th General Order).

Quonset Hut
Temporary buildings created in 1941 and manufactured for the Navy at a facility in Quonset, RI; little more than semi-circular steel ribs with corrugated sheet metal attached to them; used for everything from troop quarters to supply sheds to airplane hangars; for many years both MCRDs used them until more permanent structures could be built; some are still in use at MCB Camp Pendleton and elsewhere.

Romeo

Salty Language

R and R

Rest and Recuperation; rest and relaxation; a respite from combat; vacation.

Rack

Bed; usually bunk beds.

Rack Ops

Sleep; also "Rack Out."

Raghead

Any Arab person; refers to the common headdress (turban) of the region.

Raiders

Marine Raider Battalions; also refers to individual Marines assigned to those units; commando-type units created during WWII to carry out specialized raids and behind-the-lines missions; 2nd Raider Battalion was commanded by LtCol Evans Carlson, and participated in the famous "Makin Island Raid"; 1st Raider Battalion was commanded by LtCol "Red Mike" Edson, and fought with distinction at Guadalcanal; the Raider Regiment was eventually disbanded and reconstituted as the 4th Marines; the Raider motto is "Gung Ho."

Railroad Tracks

Slang for the rank insignia of a "Captain of Marines."

Rank

The military authority of an individual within the structure of an organization; military rank is represented by insignia showing relative authority; rank increases in relationship to pay grade, but is distinctly different; for instance a Major of Marines should not be referred to as an O-4, and a Sergeant Major of Marines is *never* called an E-9; see "Pay Grade."

Ranking
Seniority or position within a rank unit; factors involved are date of rank and date of enlistment or commissioning; similar to precedence.

Rappel
Method of sliding down a rope to traverse steep terrain, or to descend from a hovering helicopter; see "Fast Rope."

Rat Fucked
Torn apart or rifled through; originated in Vietnam when cases of C-Rations (Rats) would be gone through and ransacked in the process of being transported to the field.

Rauber, Francis D.
Second Sergeant Major of the Marine Corps; served from Sept 1, 1959 until June 28, 1961.

Razor Wire
Similar to barbed wire or concertina, with a sharp edge on one side and spikes every inch or so.

Re-up
Reenlist or volunteer to serve another tour; term adopted from the Army; a more proper term for Marines is "Ship Over."

Recon

Reconnoiter; patrol looking for enemy movements and facilities in order to gain information; contact is usually avoided if at all possible; also to scout out *anything*.

Recon Marines

Highly trained Marines assigned to Force Recon Companies and Recon Battalions; conduct amphibious and ground reconnaissance operations, surveillance, battlespace shaping, and limited scale raids in support of a landing force; Recon Battalion motto is "Swift, Silent and Deadly."

Recruit

A person enlisted into the Marine Corps in anticipation of attending boot camp, or a person undergoing training in boot camp; must earn the title "Marine" by successfully completing boot camp; some enlistees are given rank (usually PFC or LCpl) on enlistment and are paid at that grade, but during boot camp they wear no rank and are called "Recruit" like everyone else; only upon graduation are they allowed to wear the insignia of their rank.

Recruit Punishment

Unofficial punishments given to recruits by drill instructors for minor infractions of the rules; while some of them may sound cruel, they are essentially harmless and good tools for teaching a lesson.

Recruiter

Marine who must sort through the flotsam and jetsam of American youth in order to find a few who have the mettle to be Marines; the individual who promises you will be "screwed" on a regular basis if you join the Corps.

Recruiter Assistance

Temporary duty assignment of up to 30-days to assist local recruiters by making presentations to school groups, leading poolee training, and performing general office duties; offered to recent boot camp graduates by recruiters if they believe the new Marine can be of help; also available to *all* Marines when mutually agreed upon and approved.

Recycle

Boot camp term meaning a recruit is removed from his or her platoon and placed in another platoon in order to repeat some portion of training; usually occurs because a recruit did not successfully complete a required training item, to improve a recruit's physical conditioning, or in some cases because a recruit's attitude is bad; a traumatic event, because it means the recruit will spend more time at the "MCRD."

Refil

A lifer; used at times when commanders prohibit the use of the term "lifer"; (hint… it's "lifer" spelled backwards).

Regiment
Usually an infantry or artillery unit consisting of from 4 to 6 battalions; generally commanded by a colonel; a number of regiments will make up a division.

REMF
Rear Echelon Mother Fucker; pogue; a staff person.

Remington Raider
Office personnel; the reference is to the Remington typewriter, which was widely used (a "typewriter" was a mechanical device used prior to the advent of computers to create printed pages containing words).

Repeat
A word removed from the vocabulary of artillery and mortar personnel; using the term casually can cause un-wanted action (i.e. fire the last mission again); "Say Again" is the acceptable replacement phrase.

Request Mast
Every Marine's right to be heard; at every step up the chain of command any Marine may request to see the next person in authority all the way to the Commandant of the Marine Corps; when request mast is asked for the Marine does not have to explain why, but he must make the request again at every step up the ladder; if a Marine requests mast to the CMC he had *better* have a good reason!

Reservist

Member of the "Fleet Marine Corps Reserve"; these Marines "Drill" one weekend every month and two weeks each summer after completion of boot camp and their MOS school; points are earned toward retirement, which can be taken at age 60; they can be mobilized to active duty in time of need; see "Weekend Warrior."

Retread

Usually refers to a person who gets out of the military and then comes back in.

Retreat

Bugle call sounded when the U. S. flag is being lowered at the end of the day; also something the Army (but *never* the Marine Corps) sometimes does in battle.

Retriever

A special tank (or AAV) designed as a sort of "wrecker."

Reveille

Signal to awaken, get out of bed, and begin the day; often a bugle call; in boot camp it is more often the yells and screams of Drill Instructors and the sound of GI cans crashing to the deck.

RHIP

Rank Has Its Privileges; a truism; also among lower ranking enlisted Marines, "Rank Has Its Pricks."

Salty Language

Ribbon Creek
Small river which flows through Parris Island in an area once used for field training; in 1956 six recruits died while on a training exercise here; Staff Sergeant Matthew McKeon, their Senior Drill Instructor, was court-martialed and found guilty of negligence and drinking on duty; the investigations which followed highlighted the general practices of maltreatment of recruits, and caused extensive revisions in the training program.

Riggers Tape
Duct tape; used for holding anything and everything together; sometimes called "100 MPH Tape."

Riki Tik
Quickly; right away; from an oriental phrase; used mostly in the form "Most Riki Tik."

Ring Knocker
Graduate of the Naval Academy, Military Academy or Air Force Academy; they tend to "absent-mindedly" tap the ring on bars to bring attention to it - so that everyone is aware the officer is an academy grad.

RLT
Regimental Landing Team; regiment of Marines consisting of three battalions and supporting artillery, tanks, amtracs, heavy weapons, etc.; a self-supporting force, and a concept unique to the Marine Corps.

RM
Royal Marines.

Rock
Idiot; as in "That guy is a rock."

Rock, The
Okinawa, Japan.

Rock Painter
Someone (usually a new commanding officer) who makes changes just for the sake of change; comes from the period when every Marine Corps Quonset hut had a neat border of painted rocks around the entrance; if they were white, the new CO might order them repainted red – for no good reason.

Rock and Roll
An alliteration of lock and load; it means to begin an action; to start; it also means to fire a weapon on full automatic.

Rocks and Shoals
System of Naval justice prior to the introduction of the UCMJ; also indicates an "ass chewing," as in "The Gunny just read him Rocks and Shoals."

Roger
Yes; affirmative.

ROK Marines
The fiercest of fighters in the Republic of Korea.

Romp N' Stomp
Close Order Drill.

RON
Remain Overnight; usually used by aircrews.

Rope
Former name for a female drill instructor; until they were authorized to wear the campaign cover, female Marine drill instructors were once designated by a crimson agulet worn on the left shoulder.

Rosenthal, Joseph J.
Awarded the Pulitzer Award for photography for his classic shot of Marines raising the American flag on Iwo Jima's Mount Suribachi in 1945; it is probably the most famous photograph ever taken.

Rotorhead
Helicopter pilot.

Rottencrotch, Suzy
See "Suzy Rottencrotch."

Route Step
Normal pace in marching in which it is not necessary or practical to march in step; used mainly in the field when moving from place to place as a unit.

Routine Medevac
A Marine with a very minor wound, who can wait until the more seriously wounded are evacuated; also a KIA.

Royal Marines
British Marines in the service of the Queen.

RPG
Rocket Propelled Grenade; a shoulder-fired infantry weapon; equivalent to a "LAAW."

RSO
Regional Security Officer; the representative of "DSS" at a diplomatic post overseas; the person an MSG Detachment Commander reports to in his operational "Chain of Command."

RST
Rope Suspension Training; see "Rappelling," "SPIE Rigging," and "Fast Roping."

RTO
Radio Telegraph Operator; the Marine who carries a PRC.

RTR
Recruit Training Regiment; headquarters unit of the Recruit Training Battalions; the RTR at MCRD Parris Island has four battalions (including the 4th RTBn, which is the only boot camp unit for female Marines) while the RTR at MCRD San Diego has three.

Rubber Lady
Air mattress; sometimes called a "Rubber Whore" or "Rubber Bitch."

Ruffles and Flourishes
Musical honor for general officers and equivalent ranking officials.

Rump Ranger
Homosexual.

Run Up the Bullshit Flag
Express a belief that something is false or misleading.

Run Up the Flagpole
Receive official punishment such as an "Article 15."

Russell, John H.
Sixteenth Commandant of the Marine Corps; named Major General Commandant March 1, 1934 and served until Nov. 30, 1936.

Russian Rope
See "Irish Pennant."

Salty Language

Sierra

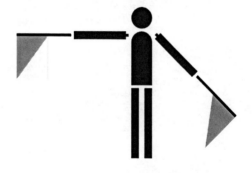

Salty Language

S-1

The administrative section or officer of a battalion.

S-2

The intelligence section or officer of a battalion.

S-3

The operations and training section or officer of a battalion.

S-4

The logistics and supply section or officer of a battalion.

Sage Green

One of the names for the color of utility uniforms; see also "OD."

Sally

Nickname for the air mattresses at one time provided to Marines for field use; see "Rubber Lady."

Sally Port

A gate or passage into a fortified place.

Salty

Referring to someone or something with a lot of experience, particularly at sea; a "Salty" Marine is one who has been around awhile; a salty uniform is more faded and obviously used, but still sharp; salty language is language salted with profanities or obscenities.

SAM
Surface to Air Missile.

Sam Browne
Leather duty belt worn by commissioned and warrant officers; consists of a belt around the waist with a second belt running from left hip over the right shoulder back to the left hip; gives added support for the wearing of a sword; worn only for special occasions such as parades and formal events.

San Diego CA
Location of the Marine Corps' west coast Recruit Depot; located in San Diego adjacent to the airport; sometimes called "Dago"; see "Hollywood Marine."

Sand Crab
A sideways-walking beach scavenger; refers to a civil service employee, or a civilian contractor aboard ship.

Sand Fleas
Parris Island pests which delight in climbing on recruits attempting to stand at attention.

Sandy
A-1 Skyraider aircraft.

SAR
Search and Rescue.

Sarge
Army diminutive of "sergeant"; a good way to get your ass kicked when talking to a "Sergeant of Marines."

SAW

M249 Squad Automatic Weapon; the automatic weapon for each fire team; it replaced the "BAR" after Vietnam.

Say Again

Repeat what you just said; particularly important when talking to an artillery or mortar unit on the radio; "Repeat" has specific consequences (fire again).

Scarlet and Gold

Official colors of the U. S. Marine Corps as ordered by Major General Commandant John A. Lejeune in 1921.

School of Infantry

MOS school for the Infantry career field; SOI East is at Camp Lejeune, and SOI West is at Camp Pendleton; every Marine graduating from boot camp goes next to SOI; new Marines who have not been assigned an 0300 (Infantry) MOS report to Marine Combat Training (MCT) for four weeks of intensive training in combat weapons and techniques because "Every Marine is a Rifleman"; new Infantry Marines report to the School of Infantry's "Infantry Training Battalion" for MOS training.

School Circle

Informal circle, sitting or standing around a Drill Instructor or other instructor, for the purpose of receiving training.

Scoop
Information; usually unofficial, but often correct; see "Bum Scoop."

Screw the Pooch
Make a major mistake, particularly one which will have serious ramifications.

Scribe
Recruit who takes notes and makes lists for the platoon and drill instructors; an informal position selected by the drill instructors.

Scrounge
Unofficial "scavenger hunt" for parts and equipment; when the supply system doesn't come through, it's time to "scrounge" up what you need; someone who is particularly good at locating items is called a "scrounger."

Scumbag
See "Shitbird" or "Maggot."

Scuttlebutt
(*n*) Keg of water or water fountain aboard ship around which sailors gather to swap tales and gossip; (*v*) presently used for unverified information passed informally (often around the water fountain).

Scuz Brush
Cleaning brush included in a recruit's PX issue; used for cleaning the deck.

SDO

Staff (or Squadron) Duty Officer; the representative of the commander during non-duty hours.

Sea Bat

Mythical creature used in a practical joke by salty Marines and sailors against inexperienced compatriots while aboard ship; there are a number of permutations, some quite nasty; one takes place when a newbie is shown a helmet lying on the deck - he is told that someone has captured a sea bat, and that it is trapped under the helmet; the victim is told to position himself with one hand on either side of the helmet, so that when it lifted he can capture the bat with his hands; the "bat" turns out to be a pile of feces or some other equally repulsive substance.

Sea Buoy

See "Mail Buoy."

Sea Dip

Effect achieved by over-tightening the hoop in a "Barracks Cover," causing the sides to curve downward; a sign of "Saltiness"; sometimes considered fashionable among enlisted Marines; never done by any officer other than a "Mustang," and then only with great subtlety.

Sea Lawyer

Someone who appears to know all the angles and methods to escape punishment; a person providing legal advice who is not a lawyer.

Sea Snake
Legendary creature which newer crew members are sent to find; also has a cousin in areas where cold weather training is conducted – the "*Snow* Snake."

Sea Story
A tale; often contains a small grain of truth somewhere.

Seabag
Large canvas bag into which sailors and Marines stuff their entire issue of uniforms and personal items when being transferred; in the Army it is called a "Duffel Bag."

Seabag Drag
Being transferred, shipping out or moving to new quarters; from the act of dragging the sea bag from place to place.

Seabees
Navy Combat Construction Battalions; from initials "CB."

Seagoing Bellhop
Derogatory term for "Marines"; used by those who are jealous of the Marine "Dress Blue" uniform.

Seagoing Marine
The first mission of the Marine Corps; Marines were once trained at "Sea School" and assigned to a Marine Detachment aboard ship; while most Marines will at some time in their career spend time aboard

ship, only those assigned as members of the ship's compliment earned this title; the insignia of a seagoing Marine is a gold seahorse superimposed on a gold anchor within a crimson lozenge; in 1998 all Marine shipboard detachments were disbanded, thus ending a tradition which dated to 1775.

SEAL

Sea, Air, Land; special operations force of the U. S. Navy; quite possibly the most overrated unit in the armed forces; also an aquatic mammal which delights audiences by balancing a ball on its nose while clapping its fins; the differences between the two types are quite subtle.

Secretary of the Navy

Civilian appointee of the President responsible for the efficient management of the Navy and Marine Corps; reports to the Secretary of Defense; abbreviated "SecNav."

Second Lieutenant

First grade of commissioned officer; indicated by a gold bar on the collar or epaulet of the uniform; pay grade is O-1; see "Butter Bar."

Secure

To stop work; to lock something up for safe keeping; to capture an objective; to make safe, as in "secure an LZ."

Selection Board

Panel which selects Marines for promotion; also called a "Promotion Board."

Semper Fidelis
Latin for "Always Faithful"; current motto of the Marine Corps; often expressed informally as "Semper Fi."

Semper Fi, Mac
An "Old Corps" greeting which could mean most anything between Marines; it was all in *how* and *when* it was said.

Semper Gumby
Unofficial motto of the Marine Corps; a mixture of Latin and cartoon dialects meaning "Always Flexible."

Senior Drill Instructor (SDI)
See "Drill Instructor."

Seniority Number
Number assigned to a SNCO selected for promotion which illustrates the Marine's relative standing or seniority in comparison to other Marines selected to the same pay grade at the same time.

Sergeant
Virtually any NCO (E-5 and up) in the Army or Air Force; often shortened to "Sarge."

Sergeant Major of Marines
Senior enlisted person in a battalion, regiment, group, wing or higher; insignia consists of three chevrons and four rockers with a star between the chevrons and rockers; pay grade is E-9 (same as a master gunnery sergeant).

Sergeant Major of the Marine Corps
A *billet*, not a rank; the senior enlisted advisor to the Commandant of the Marine Corps; insignia is the same as a sergeant major, except that between the chevrons and rockers is an eagle, globe and anchor flanked by two stars; pay grade is E-9 (same as sergeants major and master gunnery sergeants).

Sergeant of Marines
Second step in the noncommissioned officer ranks; indicated by three chevrons with crossed rifles; pay grade is E-5.

Service Stripe
See "Hash Mark."

SGLI
Servicemen's Group Life Insurance; military life insurance.

Shake and Bake
See "Napalm."

Shanghai
Hijack; term originally used by the "China Marines."

Shellback
Anyone who has crossed the Equator and gone through the initiation; all others are mere "Polliwogs."

Shelter Half
Half of a pup tent; each Marine carried one half so that two Marines could buddy up, snap or button their shelter halves together, and make a complete tent.

Shepherd, Lemuel C. Jr.
Twentieth Commandant of the Marine Corps; served from Jan 1, 1952 until Dec 31, 1955 in the rank of general.

Ship
Large vessel equipped for deep-water operation; not to be confused with a boat; see "Boat."

Ship's Compliment
Sailors and Marines who make up the permanent party of a ship, as opposed to those who are assigned for a single cruise or action; see "Seagoing Marine."

Shield, The
Subdued metal collar device worn by medical corpsmen below the rank of chief petty officer while in field uniform; worn on the left collar, while rank insignia is worn on the right; properly called a "Caduceus."

Ship Over
Reenlist.

Shit Bird
A screw-up; someone who regularly gets into trouble, or whose uniform routinely looks like a "Soup Sandwich"; often simply called a "Bird."

Shit Hot
The best; in prime form.

Shit List
Any unofficial list you *don't* want to be on.

Shit Load

A lot; boo-coo.

Shit Paper

Toilet paper; sometimes called "John Wayne Paper" because it's rough, and tough, and doesn't take shit off of *anybody!*

Shit Pot

Toilet; also a large group, as in "There's a whole shit-pot full of them!"

Shit Sandwich

A bad or barely tolerable event; usually a mission or activity that has gone bad; as in, "We're in a real shit sandwich now!"

Shitcan

(*n*) trash can; (*v*) to throw something away; to remove a person from his or her position; fire; relieve of duty.

Shithook

A pejorative term for the CH-47 Chinook helicopter.

Shitter

Toilet; also a nickname given to CH-53 helicopters due to the huge amounts of exhaust smoke they "shit" out of their exhausts; see "Super Shitter."

Shit the Bed

Break down; become inoperable.

Shock Troop

Form of address between Marines, mostly in-country during Vietnam.

Short

Close to EAS or PCS; an attitude involving lack of interest and inattention; someone who is short is known as a "Short Timer."

Short Arm Inspection

Physical inspection of the genitals, usually by a corpsman; often done in formation following "Cinderella Liberty" in a foreign port; intended to identify the early signs of sexually transmitted diseases so they could be treated properly; see "Pecker Checker."

Short Round

Artillery shell which falls short of its intended target, often because of defective gunpowder or a miscalculation; also a diminutive person.

Short Timer

Anyone nearing the end of an enlistment or assignment.

Shoup, David M.

Medal of Honor recipient and twenty-second Commandant of the Marine Corps; served from Jan 1, 1960 until Dec 31, 1963.

Shower Shoes

"Flip flops" worn in communal showers for sanitary reasons; also someone who hasn't been in the military long enough to be classified as a "Boot" yet.

Sick Bay

Location on a ship or in a unit area where sick and injured personnel are treated; see "BAS."

Sick Bay Commando
Someone who is frequently at sick call; a malingerer; see "Laminated Light Duty Chit."

Sick Call
Designated time and place for people to report themselves as sick and unable to perform their duties.

Sierra Hotel
Shit Hot; the best; in prime form.

Sight Alignment
Aligning the rear and front sights of a weapon.

Sight Picture
Placing your target directly upon the front sight blade of a weapon once proper "Sight Alignment" had been acquired.

Signal Bridge
Small open deck on the superstructure of a ship, usually above the bridge, for the hoisting of flags and pennants used to signal to other ships and shore installations.

Silent Drill Platoon (or Team)
The preeminent practitioners of "Close Order Drill"; perform a program of intricate movements without a single verbal command; they are absolutely unfuckingbelievable!

Single Digit Midget
A "short-timer" with less than 10 days remaining on his enlistment contract or overseas tour; sometimes called a "One Digit Midget."

Sinville.
See "Kin Ville."

Six
Usually "Your Six" or "Your Six O'Clock" meaning your back; from the clock system of identifying an object; when 12 is to your front, 6 is to your rear.

Six, Six and a Kick
Punishment consisting of 6 months forfeiture of pay, 6 months confinement at hard labor, and a dishonorable discharge.

Six, The
Commanding Officer; designation usually used during radio transmissions.

Six-By
Truck with six-wheel drive; a deuce and a half.

Skate
(*v*) Perform easy duty, or just "goof off"; (*n*) a Marine who is always "hiding and sliding."

Skinny
Information; usually accurate; when it is *known* to be accurate it is often called "Straight Skinny"; the term originated back in the days when typewriters were used and info could be gleaned from the thin pieces of carbon paper found in the "Shitcan"; see also "Scoop."

Skipper
Term of respect for a company grade officer (usually a captain).

Skippie
A not too bright Marine.

Skittles™
Motrin™; supposedly because Navy Corpsmen hand out the pain killer like candy; sometimes called "Infantryman's Candy" or "Vitamin M."

Skivvies
Underwear; especially baggy white boxer shorts.

Skivvy Honcho
Lothario; ladies man; someone who frequents "Skivvie Houses."

Skivvy House
Brothel; whorehouse.

Skoshi
Small space or time; from Japanese; sometimes "Skosh."

SKS
Simonov Soviet or Chinese made semiautomatic rifle; standard Viet Cong infantry rifle, with a distinctive sound and high accuracy.

Skylark
Goof off.

Sky Pilot
Chaplain.

Slack
To treat with a reduced level of emphasis; to give or "cut" someone slack; to ease off.

Slash Wire
See "Comm Wire."

Slick
Huey helicopter with the seats removed so that a larger number of combat troops could be transported (from the helicopter's slick deck); often unarmed.

Slick Sleeve
Private; so called because they wear no chevrons.

Sliders
Hamburgers, from naval reference to the amount of fat and grease on them, which allows them to slide down the throat; "With Lids" refers to cheeseburgers.

Slit Trench
See "Straddle Trench."

Slope
Also "Slopehead; see "Zip"

Slop Chute
Bar for lower enlisted grades having few amenities and serving only beer - no hard liquor.

Small Arms
Weapons of small caliber usually requiring only one person to operate, as opposed to crew-served weapons; not a precise term, as some crew-served weapons (such as smaller machineguns) are considered small arms.

Salty Language

Small Boat and Barge School
   The U. S. Naval Academy; see "Canoe U."

SMAW
   Shoulder Launched Multi-Purpose Assault Weapon; missile firing weapon which fires an 83-mm dual mode encased rocket (which detonates in either a fast mode against a hard target or a slow mode against a soft target).

SMEAC
   Acronym for a "5-Paragraph Order"; it means Situation, Mission, Execution, Administration and Logistics, and Command and Signal.

Smoker
   Boxing match.

Smoking Lamp
   When the smoking lamp is lit smoking is permitted, when it is out smoking is prohibited; from the naval phrase; in the days of wooden ships it was necessary to strictly control the use of fire and smoking materials; a lamp was hung on the forecastle, where sailors were allowed to sit and relax, and they knew it was OK to smoke their pipes if it was lit.

SNAFU
   Situation Normal, All Fucked (or Fouled) Up.

Snake
   See "Cobra"; also, a pejorative term used in the 1960s in reference to Women Marines.

Snake Pit
Living quarters of female enlisted Marines; this term traces its roots to the name British naval officers gave to the ladies' lounge at the Union Club in Valletta, Malta.

Snake Eyes
500-pound bombs dropped by jet aircraft during "CAS."

Snap and Pop
Term used to describe sharp and quick rifle drill, as would be seen when viewing the Marine Corps "Silent Drill Platoon."

Snap In
Practice, especially dry-firing on a rifle range; learn a new job.

SNCO
Staff Noncommissioned Officer; an NCO in the rank of staff sergeant, gunnery sergeant, master sergeant, first sergeant, sergeant major, master gunnery sergeant; while officially enlisted Marines, they are set apart much like commissioned officers are.

Snoopin' and Poopin'
Patrolling; conducting a reconnaissance.

Snot Locker
Nose.

Snuffy
Low ranking enlisted Marine.

SOC
Special Operations Capable; designation usually placed after the title of a Marine unit, usually within parenthesis (SOC); Marine Expeditionary Units are the best example of an organization which can be given this designation.

SOI
School of Infantry.

Sommers, David W.
Eleventh Sergeant Major of the Marine Corps; served from June 27, 1987 through June 27, 1991.

SOP
Standard Operating Procedure.

Sortie
A single mission by one aircraft.

SOS
Shit on a Shingle; breakfast meal consisting of creamed chipped beef served on toast.

Soup Cooler
Mouth.

Soup Sandwich
Not "Squared Away"; not sharp or crisp; sloppy.

Sound Off
Complain; speak; also a command for the band to play during a parade.

Sousa, John Philip
The "March King"; he was leader of the Marine Band from 1 October 1880 until 30 July 1892; Sousa wrote over 100 marches, including "The Stars and Stripes Forever" and "Semper Fidelis."

SP
Shore Patrol; duties performed by both Navy petty officers and Marine noncommissioned officers; usually an additional duty; used to police sailors and Marines on liberty in a foreign or domestic port.

Space A
Space Available; travel via a "MAC Flight."

Spad
A-1 Skyraider aircraft.

Special Sea and Anchor Detail
Shipboard situation in which everyone has a special job on entering and leaving a port; this may include "Manning the Rails."

Spider Hole
A well concealed enemy fighting hole.

SPIE Rig
Special Patrol Insertion Extraction; special heavy rope designed to be hung from a helicopter to which Marines can be attached; used to insert them into, or extract them from, dense jungle or other places where helicopters cannot land.

Spit Shine

Method of putting a high-gloss shine on footwear; no longer used on dress shoes since the advent of Corfams.

Splash

Drive an Amtrac off the back of an amphibious ship; shoot down an enemy plane, particularly over the ocean.

Splice the Main Brace

Invitation to have an alcoholic drink; originally a naval term indicating the crew should muster for their regular issue of "Grog"; the issue of Grog on U. S. flag vessels ended during the Civil War, but is still practiced in the Royal Navy; the "main brace" is the line which holds the main sail in place. It was always a target, and after a battle the first duty of most sailors was to take care of the main brace and splice it if it was torn; on completion of that arduous task it was customary to get together for a drink of strong spirits.

Split Tail

Any female.

Spot Promotion

See "Hip Pocket Promotion."

Spouse

Wife or husband; usually preceded with "Dependent."

Spooky
Flare ship; see "Basketball."

Squad
Unit consisting of a three fire teams; part of a platoon; usually led by a sergeant or staff sergeant.

Squad Bay
Living quarters for a recruit platoon; consists of a large open space where bunk beds are set up, a head, a drill instructor's hut, and a small meeting area; also any open living space for Marines.

Squared Away
In good shape; everything in place; prepared.

Squid
Sailor.

SRB
Service Record Book.

SRIG
Surveillance, Reconnaissance and Intelligence Group (now defunct, probably because nobody could spell it).

SSAN
Social Security Account Number; also "Attack Nuclear Submarine."

SSN
Social Security Number; also "Nuclear Submarine."

SSS

Shit, shower and shave; also "Skin So Soft," a skin moisturizer by Avon which also repels bugs; it works so well that it is now part of the initial PX issue in boot camp (the cost of which comes out of the recruit's first pay).

STA Platoon

Surveillance and Target Acquisition Platoon; an infantry battalion's scout/snipers.

Stacking Swivel

Clip near the muzzle of most military rifles allowing for the stacking of weapons when in garrison; also used as a euphemism for someone's "neck."

Staff Sergeant of Marines

First staff noncommissioned officer rank; indicated by three chevrons with a single rocker connecting them and crossed rifles in between chevrons and rocker; pay grade is E-6; *never* should be called "Staff" – and those who do should be expected to be beaten with one!

Stanchion

Any pole or pillar used to support the "Overhead."

Stand Fast

Command to stay where you are and not move until told otherwise; wait.

Standing Order

Order which remains in place for perpetuity.

Starboard
Right; from the naval term; the starboard side of a ship is illuminated with a green light.

Starchies
Highly starched utilities; putting on a fresh pair was called "Busting Starch" because the trouser legs would be stuck together.

Starlight Scope
Night vision equipment; see "Green Eye."

Stateside
The United States of America; during Vietnam it was also referred to as "The World," as in "Back in the World."

Static Line
(*n*) strap which is hooked to the anchor line cable in an aircraft; it deploys a jumper's parachute upon exit; (*v*) type of parachute jump where it is necessary to "hook up," as opposed to a "Freefall"; called "Dope on a Rope" by "HALO" qualified parachutists.

Steak and Eggs
Traditional pre-assault meal given to Marines before a beach landing, especially during combat operations; sometimes called "The Last Breakfast."

Steel Beach Party
Party aboard a ship; usually held on the flight deck.

Stick

An individual row or line of Marines lined up to disembark a vehicle, aircraft or ship; most famously used in reference to a group of paratroopers preparing to jump from a well maintained and fully functional aircraft.

Stow

Put something away in its assigned place; also to stop, as in the Navy phrase, "stow that bilge," meaning "stop talking garbage."

Straight Skinny

See "Skinny."

Straddle Trench

Field head or latrine dug quickly with an entrenching tool; just wide enough so that a grunt can squat with one foot on either side; also called a "Slit Trench."

Street, The

Drill Field; usually used by Drill Instructors.

Stroke Book

Pornographic magazine.

Stumps, The

Marine Corps Air-Ground Combat Center, Twenty Nine Palms, California; the largest Marine Corps Base, located in the middle of the Mojave desert; it is said that a Marine cannot go "UA" there because he can walk for three days and still be seen from "Mainside."

Salty Language

Suck

Mouth; as in, "Shut your suck."

Suck, The

See "Crotch."

Sucking Chest Wound

Chest wound involving a punctured lung; sometimes used to highlight an unpleasant situation or task, as in, "This is about as much fun as a sucking chest wound!"

Sunset Parade

Precision parade held in front of the backdrop of the "Marine Corps War Memorial"; features the music of "The Commandant's Own," The United States Marine Drum and Bugle Corps, and precision drill by the Marine Corps "Silent Drill Platoon"; open to the public at no charge; reservations are not necessary; not to be confused with the "Evening Parade."

Super Shitter

Nickname reserved specifically for the CH-53E Super Sea Stallion helicopter; see "Shitter."

Superstructure

That portion of a ship above the main deck; decks are numbered beginning with the first deck above the main weather deck, the 01 level; therefore, the 05 level is five decks above the main weather deck; the "Bridge" is located in the superstructure.

Suppression Fire
Fire directed at an enemy position to keep that position from using their own weapons; often applied to allow portions of a unit to reposition without being hit by enemy fire; frequently called "Cover Fire."

Survey
Dispose of; evaluate for value to the mission; also to replace something, as in an old or worn out item.

Suzy Rottencrotch
Every Marine's girlfriend; many are shacked up with "Jody" while the Marine is off defending his country.

Swab
Mop; also a sailor.

Swabbie
Sailor.

Swab Jockey
Sailor.

SWAG
Scientific Wild Ass Guess; sometimes a "WAG."

Swagger Stick
A short (usually under two feet) decorated stick carried by some Marine commissioned and noncommissioned officers; they have been outlawed at times by the Marine Corps; introduced by the British Royal Marines, whose leaders use them extensively; a good example was carried by Lou Gossett Jr.'s character (Gunny Foley) in the movie "Officer and a Gentleman."

Swamp Lagoon
Pejorative term for Camp Lejeune N.C.

Sweet, Herbert J.
Fourth Sergeant Major of the Marine Corps; served from July 17, 1965 until July 31, 1969.

Swinging Dick
A male individual; most often used in the phrase, "every swinging dick," meaning *everyone*.

Swoop
Term for the travel of a Marine on liberty to his or her hometown; usually a ridiculous distance from where they are assigned.

Swoop Circle
Place on base where swoop drivers met up with swoop passengers; at Camp Lejeune it was the handball courts (formerly the outdoor theater) on "Mainside" across from the 8th Marines gym.

Tango

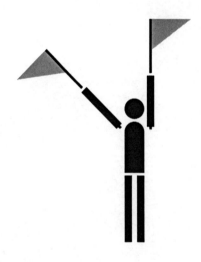

T
> See "LST."

Tacking On
> See "Pinning On."

TACP
> Tactical Air Control Party.

TAD
> Temporary Additional Duty; duty assignment in addition to one's normal billet; jokingly called "Traveling Around Drunk."

Tail End Charlie
> Last person or element in a line or column; whomever is bringing up the rear.

Tally Ho
> What pilots say upon sighting the enemy.

Tango Uniform
> Tits Up.

Tango Yankee
> Thank You.

Taps
> Lights out; last call of the day.

TBS
> The Basic School; see "Basic School."

TC
Tank Commander.

T/E
Table of Equipment; the gear a unit rates.

TECG
Tactical Exercise Control Group; the "umpires" in a training exercise; usually identified by white tape around their "Covers."

Technical Sergeant
World War II and Korea period rank; the insignia was three chevrons and two horizontal bars; it was part of a dual rank system which split technician and command ranks; became the rank of "Gunnery Sergeant" in the 1960s, at which time the crossed rifles were added.

Tell It to the Marines
Go peddle that piece of bullshit somewhere else!; used to let someone know you are not gullible, such as when a sea story is hard to believe; originated with King George of England, who would consult with his Royal Marines (who had been everywhere and done everything) when told an outlandish tale; when you use this term you are "Running Up the Bullshit Flag."

Terminal Leave
Leave from which a Marine is not expected to return to duty; taken just prior to retirement or separation; usually taken to get a jump on civilian life and/or use up any unpaid leave remaining on the books.

Tet
Vietnam Lunar New Year celebration; marked the start of an offensive by the North Vietnamese Army in 1968 to oust Americans from Vietnam; while fighting was fierce, is was a failure for the communist forces.

Teufelhunden
German for "Devil Dogs."

TDY
Army/Air Force version of "TAD."

Things on the Springs
See "Junk on the Bunk."

Thrash Light
Illumination of a combat zone by dropping 55-gal. barrels full of napalm from CH-53 helicopters.

Three Ss
Shit, shower and shave.

Tie-Tie
Length of cord with two clips every 10 inches issued to recruits; recruit would cut between the clips and use the resulting length of cord to tie laundry to a line to dry; clothes pins were not used in boot camp in the mid-20th Century; also any drawstring on a garment or piece of gear.

TIG
Time in Grade.

Tight Jawed
Pissed off; angry.

TINS
"This Is No Shit!"; sort of the "Once Upon a Time" of "Sea Stories."

TIS
Time in Service.

Tits Up
Dead, broken, inoperative; a politically correct version is "Toes Up"; also "Tango Uniform" and "Shit the Bed."

TLA
Temporary Lodging Allowance.

TMO
Traffic Management Office; where one goes to arrange for shipment of household goods, vehicles or other items in conjunction with a permanent change of station.

T/O
Table of Organization; personnel billets rated by a unit.

To the Colors
Bugle call sounded in the morning as the U. S. flag is being raised.

Toe Chain
The smaller of two chains holding dog tags; it could be draped on the big toe to identify a casualty, while the tag on the larger chain went to Graves Registration.

Toilet Seat
Pejorative term for the "Marksman" shooting badge; the lowest of three levels of marksmanship qualification; the badge is shaped like a square target; qualifications for the Marksman shooting badge would earn an "Expert" rating in the *other* services; also called a "Pizza Box."

Tombstone Brigadier General
Following World War I Congress passed a law which, upon retirement, advanced a Navy commander who had been decorated during the war one grade on the retired list. It was intended as a one-time fix for a decorated officer whose career was compromised by an accident which kept him from promotion. The law, which applied only to the Naval Service, remained in effect until 1967 when it was repealed. Marines who retired and had received personal decorations were routinely promoted to the next rank the day after retirement. The effect was most noticeable with colonels who, the day following retirement, became "Flag Officers."

Toolies
See "Bush."

Tootsie Roll

Candy which was air-dropped to Marines cut off at the Chosin Reservoir during the Korean War. It kept many of the Marines from starving to death, since all of the other food they had required heating due to the 30 degrees below zero temperatures. Tootsie Rolls could be put inside clothing, and would thaw out enough that they could be eaten. In addition, Marines would repair holes in shot up trucks and jeeps by placing a chewed up Tootsie Roll into the hole, where it would immediately freeze and create a weld.

Top

Master Sergeant; once applied to First Sergeants, but it is now a *major* faux pas to do so.

Topside

The deck or floor(s) above; from the naval term; also used to refer to the upper levels of the chain of command.

TOT

Time on Target; estimated time of arrival; the time aircraft expect to deliver their ordnance; also a preplanned mortar or artillery barrage set to occur at a specific time.

TOW

Tube-launched, Optically-tracked, Wire-guided Anti-tank missile; big brother to the "Dragon."

Toys for Tots
Nationwide project to collect toys and distribute them at Christmas to children of need; it began within the Marine Corps Reserve, and is now assisted by the Marine Corps League; it has been placed within its own corporation, the "Toys for Tots Foundation."

Track Lube
Tanker term for infantrymen.

Tractor Rat
Amtrac crewman.

TRAP
Tactical Recovery of Aircraft and Personnel; the recovery of USAF Captain Scott O'Grady by Marines in the Balkans was a good example of a TRAP mission.

Triangle
Civilian community outside MCB Quantico, VA.

TRICARE
Managed health care program for the military, dependents and retirees; replaced CHAMPUS.

Trops
Tropical Uniform consisting of Khaki Long Sleeve Shirt, Trousers, Cover & Tie; worn until the mid-1970s.

Troop and Stomp
Drill; march.

Truck
Object on top of a flagpole; it can be either a ball or an eagle, and has a pulley for the lanyard so the flag can be hoisted and lowered.

Tun Tavern
Tavern in Philadelphia where the first Marines were recruited for service in 1775; the birthplace of the Corps.

Tuna Boat Driver
A pejorative term used by tankers in reference to "Amtrac" drivers.

Turkey Bar
Bar in Okinawa or mainland Japan where oral sex is performed for a fee; in the 1960s some of the bars even advertised being Turkey Bars on their signs; the bar girls were called "Gobblers."

Turn to
Naval command to begin work.

Twilight Cruise
Last assignment prior to retirement; sometimes involves a transfer to a cushy duty station.

Twinkie
Marine aviation personnel; used during the Korean War.

Uniform

Salty Language

UA

Unauthorized Absence; the Marine Corps equivalent of "AWOL."

UAV

Unmanned Aerial Vehicle; basically a remote controlled model airplane carrying a camera; used to reconnoiter dangerous terrain.

UCMJ

Uniform Code of Military Justice; the laws governing conduct in the military; when it was introduced in the 1940s to replace the "Rocks and Shoals" system of naval justice it was jokingly said to be a way to "bring the guilty bastards in and give them a *fair* trial."

UD

Undesirable Discharge; ranks between "General" and "Bad Conduct" Discharge; also, "Uniform of the Day."

UDP

Unit Deployment Program; program where entire units are deployed to WESTPAC for periods of approximately 6 months; designed to reduce the number of unaccompanied overseas tours and improve unit continuity.

Utilities

Marine Corps fighting and field uniform; during Vietnam the Jungle Utilities (the Army called them fatigues) were introduced and eventually became "cammies," which replaced utilities.

Uncle Sam's Canoe Club
The U. S. Naval Academy (Canoe U); more broadly, the entire U. S. Navy.

Uncle Sam's Misguided Children
Alternate meaning for the acronym "USMC."

Uncle Sam's Motorcycle Club
Alternate meaning for the acronym "USMC."

U (You) Suckers Missed Christmas
Alternate meaning for the acronym USMC; often used by Marines who are deployed over the holidays.

Uncover
Remove headgear; Marines never wear headgear indoors unless "under arms."

Under Arms
Equipped with a pistol, rifle, sword, or "duty belt."

Undress Blues
A term which identified the "Dress Blue" uniform worn with ribbons rather than medals; no longer used.

Unfuckingbelievable
Marine expletive similar to "YGTBSM."

Unified Commands
Units under the control of the Joint Chiefs of Staff containing elements from all of the U. S. armed forces; normally commanded by a four star general or admiral.

Uniform Code of Military Justice
The system of justice for the military services; a federal law enacted by Congress; replaced the "Rocks and Shoals" system of justice practiced previously in the naval service.

Uniformed Services
The five armed services (Army, Navy, Air Force, Marine Corps and Coast Guard) plus the commissioned corps of the U. S. Public Health Service and the U. S. Coast and Geodetic Survey.

UNITAS
Latin word for "unity"; an annual deployment to South America which allows Marines to train with the forces of several other countries; every other year the deployment also travels to Africa.

Unit One
Field Medical Kit carried by Navy Hospital Corpsmen.

Unq
Unqualified (Pronounced *unk*); see "Non-Qual."

Unsat
Unsatisfactory.

USFSPA
Uniformed Services Former Spouses' Protection Act; law which allows a retired service member's pay to be divided with a former spouse; one of the most unfair laws ever enacted by Congress.

Utility Uniform
   Field uniform of Marines prior to the adoption of cammies; it was an olive drab shirt and trousers with a khaki Marine belt and combat boots.

Victor

Salty Language

VA

Department of Veterans Affairs; a federal cabinet department; formerly the Veterans Administration; the abbreviation DVA is *not* appropriate.

Vandegrift, Alexander A.

Eighteenth Commandant of the Marine Corps and recipient of the Medal of Honor; the hero of Guadalcanal; appointed Commandant of the Marine Corps as a lieutenant general on Jan 1, 1944; a March 21, 1945 law permitted the President to appoint the Commandant to the rank of general, which he did effective that date; an Act of Congress on Aug 7, 1947 fixed the rank of the Commandant at general.

VBIED

Vehicle Borne Improvised Explosive Device; see "IED."

VC

Vietcong; Viet Communist; see "Charlie."

VFR

Visual Flight Rules; see "IFR."

Victor Charlie

Radio talk for "Vietcong."

Vice

See "Mister Vice."

Ville

A hamlet or larger village.

Salty Language

Whiskey

Salty Language

WAG
Wild Assed Guess; usually called a "SWAG."

Waiver
Exception to a particular policy, i.e. an "Age Waiver."

Walking Dead
The 1st Battalion, 9th Marine Regiment; Marine battalion (unsuccessfully) targeted for annihilation by the "NVA."

Wall, The
Monument in Washington D.C. which lists the names of all soldiers, sailors, airmen and Marines who died during the Vietnam War.

Wall-to-Wall Counseling
Nonverbal form of counseling in which the miscreant is for all intents and purposes "taken behind the woodshed."

Wannabee
Someone who "wants to be" something or other; they usually don't have what it takes to actually "be."

Wardroom
Officers' living room and dining area aboard ship.

Warrant
Formal document authorizing a Marine's promotion; in the case of enlisted Marines, it is usually read in formation in front of the entire unit; it begins, "To all

who shall see these presents, greeting. Know Ye that reposing special trust and confidence in the fidelity and ability of...", officers are generally promoted in the privacy of the Commanding Officer's office.

Warrant Officer
An officer who ranks below a second lieutenant, but above all enlisted personnel; most warrant officers are former enlisted; they wear the insignia of first and second lieutenants, with various red stripes painted on the insignia; see "Chief Warrant Officer."

Warrior Breakfast
Meal served to recruits upon completion of the grueling 54 hour "Crucible."

Wasted
Extremely drunk; killed.

Watching TV
A series of very uncomfortable positions into which a recruit is put as a form of "Recruit Punishment."

Water Buffalo
A water tank on wheels.

Weather (whether) Leave
"Leave" taken "whether or not" it is granted by the CO; see "Unauthorized Absence."

Weekend Warrior
Reservist.

Well Deck
Lower deck on some ships which can be flooded to embark and debark Marines using amphibious tractors and boats.

WESTPAC
Western Pacific deployment.

Wetting Down
A party held to celebrate a promotion involved copious amounts of alcoholic beverages; the newly appointed Marine traditionally puts a sum equal to his monthly pay raise on the bar for the enjoyment of all.

Whale Shit
According to many Drill Instructors, the *only* thing on earth lower than a recruit - since it resides on the bottom of the ocean.

Wharton, Franklin
Third Commandant of the Marine Corps; named Lieutenant Colonel Commandant on March 7, 1804 and served until his death on Sept 1, 1818.

Whiskey 95
A type of transfer from an overseas assignment where the Marine is within three months of discharge; rather than assign him to a unit for such a short time, the Marine is assigned to a holding unit at Camp Pendleton or Camp Lejeune.

White Hat
Enlisted sailor; from the headgear worn with the enlisted uniform; see "Dixie Cup."

Whitewalls
See "High and Tight."

WIA.
Wounded in Action.

Widow Maker
Unofficial and uncomplimentary name for the CH-53 helicopter.

Wigged Out
Crazy; flipped out; "Dinky Dau."

WILCO
Will Comply; once used after "'Roger"; now archaic.

Willie Peter (WP)
White phosphorus; incendiary material which burns hot and is not extinguished with water; used in WP hand grenades and artillery rounds for marking targets in dense foliage.

Willie Peter Bag
Waterproofed canvas bag originally designed to keep a rolled up sleeping bag dry.

Wilson, Louis H.
Medal of Honor recipient and twenty-sixth Commandant of the Marine Corps; served as Commandant from July 1, 1975 until June 30, 1979.

Winchester
Term used when an aircraft runs out of ammunition.

Wing
Usually "Air Wing," an aviation unit equivalent to an infantry division; can also be used in reference to the entire Marine Corps aviation establishment.

Wing Wiper
Marine assigned to an aviation unit.

Winger
Marine assigned to the "Wing"; see "Wing Wiper."

Wings of Gold
The pilot wings of a Naval Aviator.

Wire Dog
Wireman; a Marine who lays slash wire and operates field telephones.

WM
Abbreviation for Woman Marine; no longer officially in use because women are now (supposedly) fully integrated into the Corps; acceptable for use from 1948 when women were first accepted into the regular Marine Corps, until the late 1990s when it was decreed they would be "Marines" (without prefix); also said to mean "Waste of Money"; they are also called "BAMs," Snakes" and "Devil Dykes."

Wookie Monster
Woman Marine.

Word, The
Information supposedly received from a reliable source; also "scoop," "poop," and "skinny."

World, The
The United States of America.

World of Shit
In *big* trouble.

WR
Abbreviation for Women's Reserve, used from the time women were first allowed to join the Marine Corps Reserve on Feb. 13, 1943 until 1947 when they were allowed to join the active Marine Corps.

WTFO
What The Fuck, Over?; used as a statement of disbelief, or as a question; when using radio communication terminology, it is expressed as "Whiskey Tango Foxtrot."

X-Ray

X-Ray

A watertight condition aboard ship in which certain hatches must remain closed to ensure the watertight integrity of the individual compartments.

X-Ring

Small ring inside a bull's eye; used for competition level shooting.

XO

Executive Officer; second in command; sometimes used in reference to a Marine's spouse.

Salty Language

Yankee

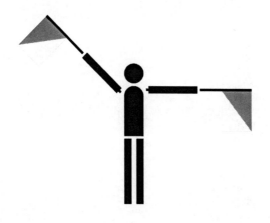

Salty Language

Yankee Station
One of two positions typically occupied by aircraft carriers off the coast of Vietnam; Yankee was the northern station responsible for disruption of commerce and logistics.

YATYAS
You Ain't Tracks, You Ain't Shit; the cryptic rallying cry of "Amtrackers."

Yemassee, S.C.
Small town west of Parris Island along the Atlantic Southern railroad mainline; for many Marines from WWI to Vietnam this was where they spent their first day in the Corps while awaiting transportation by "Cattle Car" or bus.

YGTBSM
You've Got To Be Shitting Me; a Marine's expression of disbelief; also "YBTBFSM."

Yo Yo Cord
Communications cord connecting a tanker's helmet to the intercom and radio.

You
See "Ewe."

Young Marines
Program for young people from 8-18; sponsored and run by the Marine Corps League.

Salty Language

Zulu

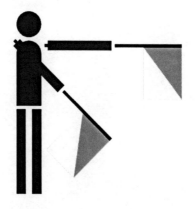

Salty Language

Zap

Shoot; hit with a bullet.

Zeilin, Jacob

Seventh Commandant of the Marine Corps; became Colonel Commandant on June 10, 1864 following the death of Harris and served until Oct 31, 1876; became the first Brigadier General Commandant, and was responsible for the creation and adoption of the Eagle, Globe and Anchor emblem of the U. S. Marine Corps.

Zero

To set the sights of a weapon so that a proper sight picture will obtain a bull on the rifle range; also an officer (taken from the pay grades "O-1" to "O-10"); also a Japanese aircraft during World War II.

Zero Dark Thirty

Very early in the morning (pronounced either *oh-dark-thirty* or *zero-dark-thirty*); also "Oh Dark Thirty."

Zip

Vietnamese; any Asian.

Zipper Head

Vietnamese; any Asian.

Zippo

Cigarette lighter prized by military personnel because of their rugged construction and ability to stay lit in a typhoon; also a nickname for a flame-thrower tank.

Zoomie
Marines assigned to an aviation unit, especially pilots; all members of the Air Force.

Zulu Time
Greenwich Mean Time; the current time at the Royal Observatory on the Prime Meridian in Greenwich England; used as a time standard worldwide; during World War II the world was divided into 24 time zones, and each was assigned a letter (minus "I" and "O"); "Z" was assigned to Greenwich, and the zone to the east was "A."

Zuni
Five-inch "FFAR" used for ground support missions.

ABOUT THE AUTHOR

Andy Bufalo retired from the Marine Corps as a Master Sergeant in January of 2000 after more than twenty-five years service. A communicator by trade, he spent most of his career in Reconnaissance and Force Reconnaissance units but also spent time with Amtracs, Combat Engineers, a reserve infantry battalion, and commanded MSG Detachments in the Congo and Australia.

He shares the view of Major Gene Duncan, who once wrote "I'd rather be a Marine private than a civilian executive." Since he is neither, he has taken to writing about the Corps he loves. He currently resides in Tampa, Florida.

Semper Fi!

Lightning Source UK Ltd.
Milton Keynes UK
18 September 2010

160080UK00006B/5/P